# The Geography Drawing Series

# Drawing Around the World
# USA

**BOOKS PUBLISHED BY BROOKDALE HOUSE:**

<u>The Write from History Series: A Charlotte Mason Curriculum</u>
(Elementary writing curriculum, teaching writing with narration, copywork, and studied dictation.
Level 1 is available for students in grades 1 to 3. Level 2 is available for students in grades 3 to 5.)

<u>The Write from Ancient History books</u>
<u>The Write from Medieval History books</u>
<u>The Write from Early Modern History Books</u>
<u>The Write from Modern History Books</u>

*<u>The Fun Spanish Level 1</u>*
(Introductory Spanish workbook for elementary students)

*<u>Sheldon's</u>* New *<u>Primary Language Lessons</u>*
(Introductory grammar workbook for elementary students)

*<u>The Westminster Shorter Catechism Copybook</u>*
(Available in the following: traditional, modern, italic, and vertical, both print and cursive)

*<u>Bible Memorization Made Easy</u>*
(Memorize Galatians, Memorize Philippians, Memorize Psalms for Praying,
and Memorize the Sermon on the Mount.)

*<u>Writing from Rhetoric Book 1</u>*
A middle school writing curriculum

To learn more about the educational products available from Brookdale House, please visit us at
**www.brookdalehouse.com** or scan

ISBN 978-1-940282-49-7

## TABLE OF CONTENTS

*Drawing Around the World: USA* is another book in The Geography Drawing Series. This series is designed to teach children to draw, from memory, large sections of the world. In *Drawing Around the World: USA*, students learn to draw, from memory, the United States of America.

## THE METHOD

Each week students study one or more new states. As they do so, they become familiar with the shape of the new states by tracing them, locating them on a map, and labeling them. To give students an opportunity to learn interesting facts about each individual state, they are asked to complete a state fact table, documenting each states' capital, area, population, and more.

To complete the table, students may research the individual states by studying a world atlas or one of several online resources; a couple of which are listed below:

50states.com Information on the states and capitals

http://www.50states.com/

Sheppard Software · USA geography games and information

http://www.sheppardsoftware.com/web_games.htm

To streamline the completion of the state fact table, instructors may prefer to purchase **The National Geographic Kids United States Atlas.** With this resource, students will find an alphabetical listing of states that provides, for each state, information to complete the State Facts Table.

To help students learn the names and relative positions of the states, students are asked to illustrate, from memory, the individual states and their locations.

Although this is a geography curriculum that utilizes drawing, it is not a drawing curriculum in the traditional sense. Students are not expected to recreate the states to scale, nor are they expected to perfectly recreate the shapes of the states.

Students are expected to learn the states and be able to create a map that demonstrates their knowledge of the states' relative positions.

Upon completion of this program, students will be more intimately familiar with the United States. They will be able to draw many of the states, from memory, and they will have a greater understanding of the position of the states, relative to one another.

**Day 1:**    Study the New State.
             Complete the State Fact Table.
             Locate and label each new state onto the dashed, black and white map.
             Draw all states studied thus far.

---

**Day 2:**    Locate and label each new state onto the dashed, black and white map.
             Draw all states studied thus far.

---

**Day 3**:    Locate and label each new state onto the dashed, black and white map.
             Draw all states studied thus far.

---

**Day 4:**    List, from memory, the states studied thus far.
             Using the blank textbox, draw, also from memory, all of the states you
             have learned.

(To incorporate timed drills, replace either the Day 3 or Day 4 map drawing with a timed drill. See the following page for guidelines on completing timed drills.)

### Coloring Pencils

Have students use coloring pencils to color as well as trace the countries on the dashed, black and white map. (Days 1, 2, 3, or 4.)

### Drawing Fun Pictures

On Day 1 encourage students to make a picture out of the individual state drawing. This will help many students to remember the shapes of the individual states.

### Timed Drills

Drills are an extremely effective practice. Drills can help children memorize large amounts of material in a short amount of time. When engaged in timed drills, children often consider the activity to be more challenging and more fun.

### General Guidelines for Timed Drills:

- Encourage students to compete against themselves.
- Even though students haven't learned all of the states in the text, start timed drills of all of the United States. Give each student a completed map to use as a guide and source of information during the drill.
  - By engaging in timed drills over states they haven't yet studied, early engagement with the material introduces students, in a fun manner, to new material.
  - Eventually students will find it easier and faster to draw the map from memory rather than by referring to the completely labeled map.
- Timed drills should always be fun and relaxed. For students that stress over the activity, remind them of the learning objective.
- When students are ready, remove the completely labeled map, and conduct a timed drill that requires students to draw and label the map from memory.

Note: Conduct the first few drills without a timer. This will help you determine how much time to give students during timed drills.

## Individual State Drawings

Each time a new state is introduced, students are asked to trace the new state and then recreate a freehand sketch of the new state. Each state is presented in a textbox. For an example, below is an illustration of the state of Louisiana.

## Dashed Black and White USA Map

Three days a week students are encouraged to locate, trace, and label all of the states they have learned onto the dashed, black and white map provided.

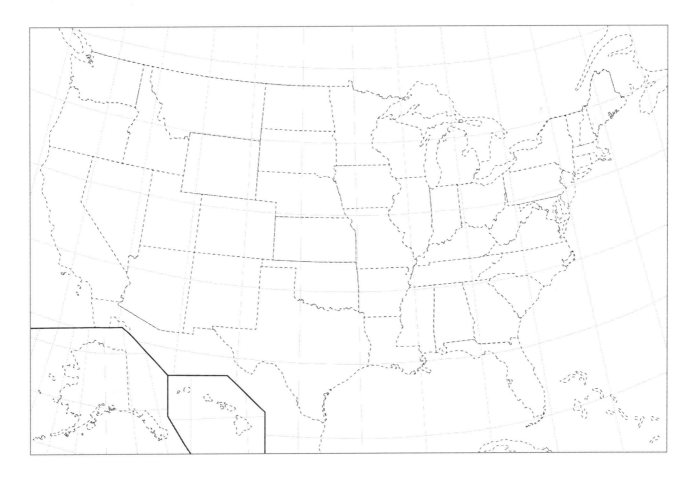

## Frame Map

After tracing and labeling the new state onto the dashed black and white map, students are asked to draw, from memory, all states they have studied onto the frame map. The black and white frame map is a blank map of the United States. The latitude and longitude lines are provided as well as the bordering countries of Mexico and Canada. Students must provide the missing states.

If students cannot remember how to complete the frame map from memory, they are encouraged to refer to the maps of the United States located on page vii.

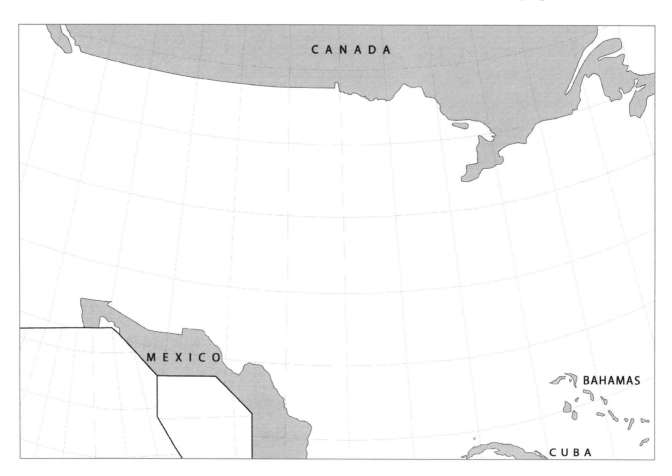

## Final Map from Memory—Blank Textbox

On Day four, students are asked to list from memory, the states they have studied. After completing the list, they recreate, also from memory, all that they have learned. For this illustration, nothing is provided except an area in which they may demonstrate their knowledge.

## Drawing the Individual States:

As your students learn to draw the individual states, you may find that they need additional practice. To help them, you may find that plastic sheet protectors or pockets and dry erase markers are a fast, fun, easy, and inexpensive way to give your students more practice drawing.

To use the sheet protectors, place the day's work in sheet protectors, and encourage your students to use dry erase markers to complete the drawings. This will allow them, with very little effort, to quickly draw and erase their illustrations several times, giving them as much practice as possible.

## Drawing States Relative to One Another:

Each week, as students learn additional states, they draw a map that includes all the states they have learned. Doing so gives students a greater understanding of the relative size of the various states and the relative position of the states.

To help students learn the proper placement of the states, latitude and longitude lines have been added to the dashed black and white maps and the frame maps, giving students reference lines that will guide them as they learn to place the states onto the maps. Sheet protectors are also helpful for this exercise.

**Memorizing the State Abbreviations and Capitals**

## State Abbreviations

If following the schedule provided on page vii, you will notice that on Day 4 students are first asked to list all of the states they have learned before drawing them onto the blank text box provided on the following page. On the small dashed line, students write, from memory, the two letter state abbreviation.

## State Capitals

To help students memorize the state capitals, each week students are asked to label both the states and the capitals.

## Running out of Labeling Space

Because many states are small on paper, students will have to draw lines from the state to the margins, so they can label the state and the capital. See the label for the state of Massachusetts on the following page, page xii.

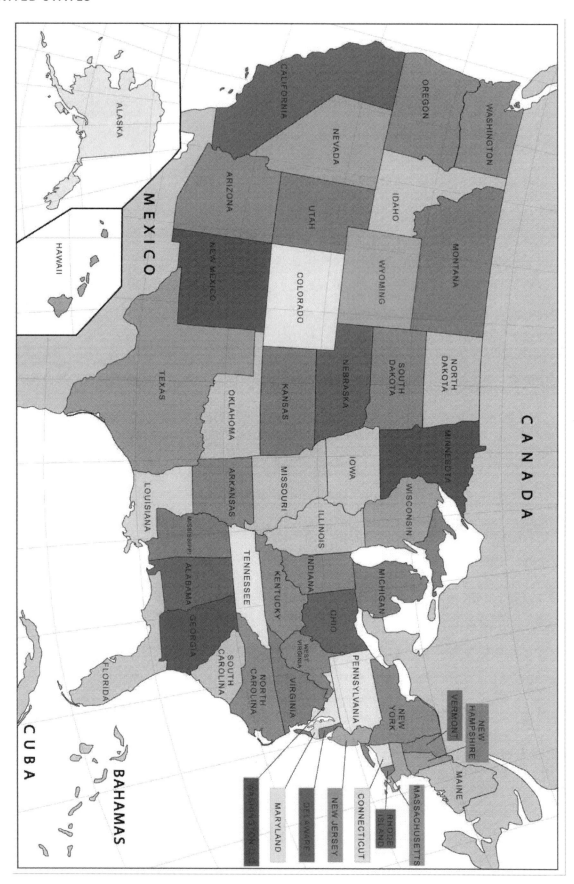

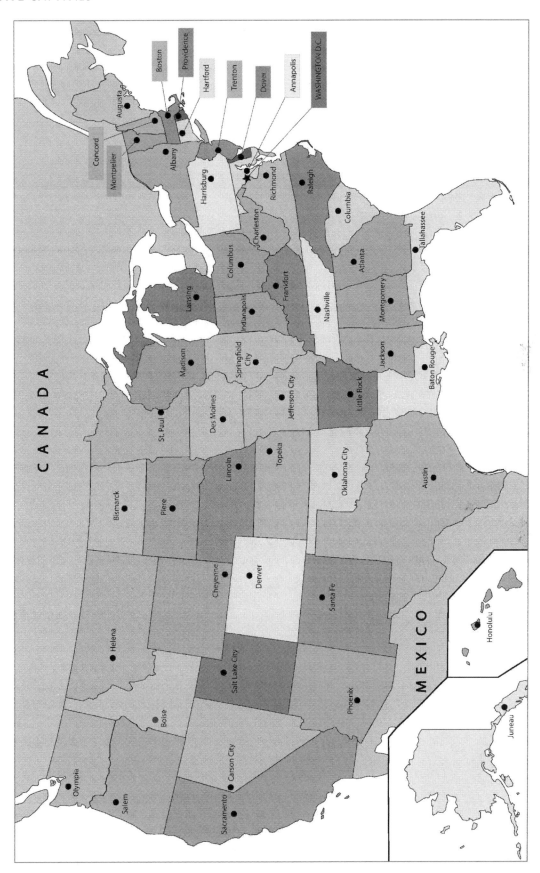

# Maine

### Trace the state.
### Draw it in the box below.

## State Facts

| Capital/Abbreviation | Agusta / ME |
|---|---|
| Area/Population | 35,387 sq.mi / 1.38 million |
| Statehood | March 15, 1820 |
| Bird/Flower | Chickadee / White pine cone & tassel |
| Industry | Paper, lumber, and wood products electric equipment, food processing leather products, texttils, tourism |
| Interesting Fact | Maine is the single large producer of bleberries in the U.S. |

**Day 1:** On the map below, trace and label
the new state and capital (or states and capitals) you have learned.

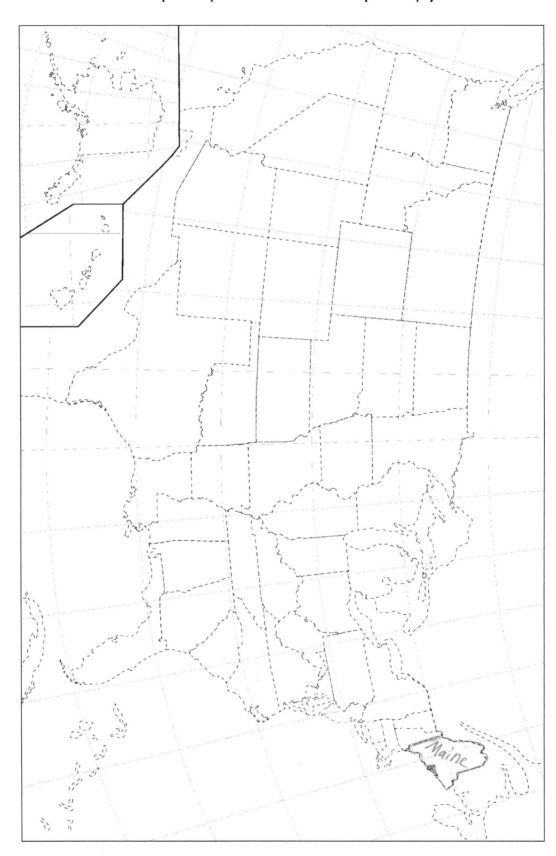

**Day 1:** On the map below, draw and label
the new state (or states) you have learned. Add the capital(s).

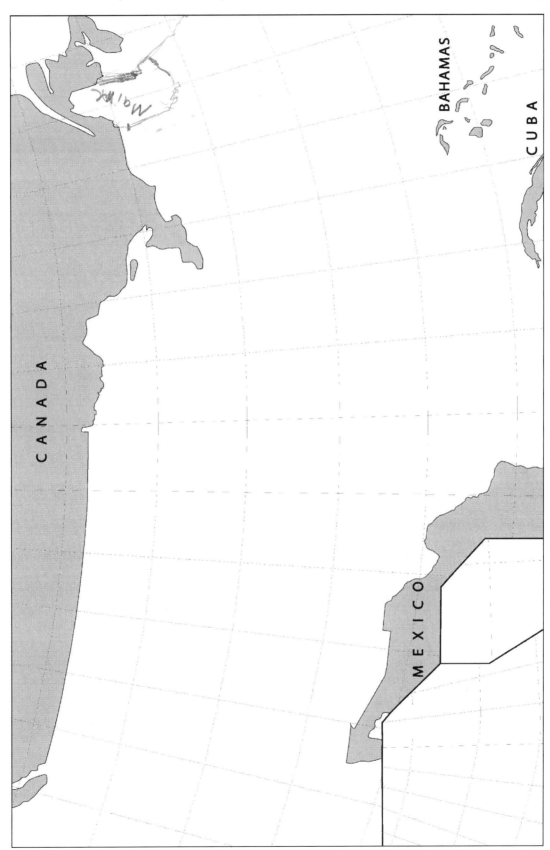

**Day 2:** On the map below, trace and label
all of the states and capitals you have learned.

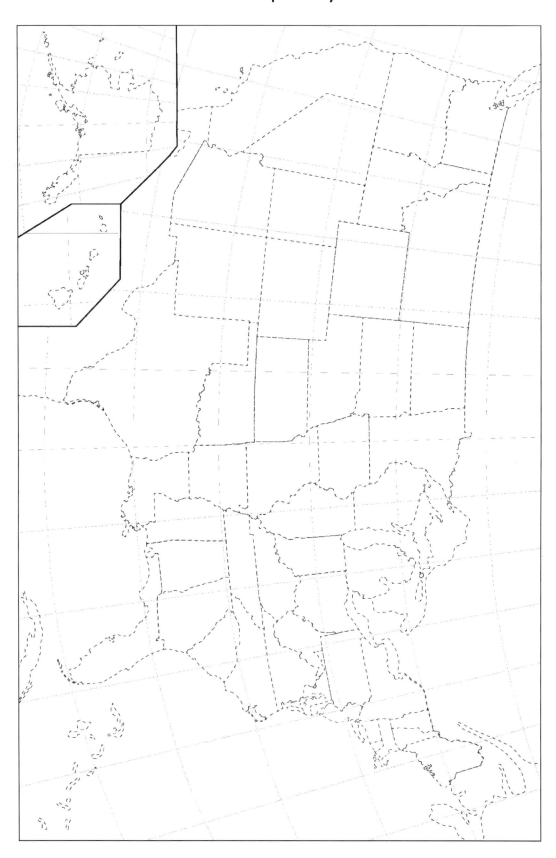

**Day 2:** On the map below, draw and label all of the states and capitals you have learned.

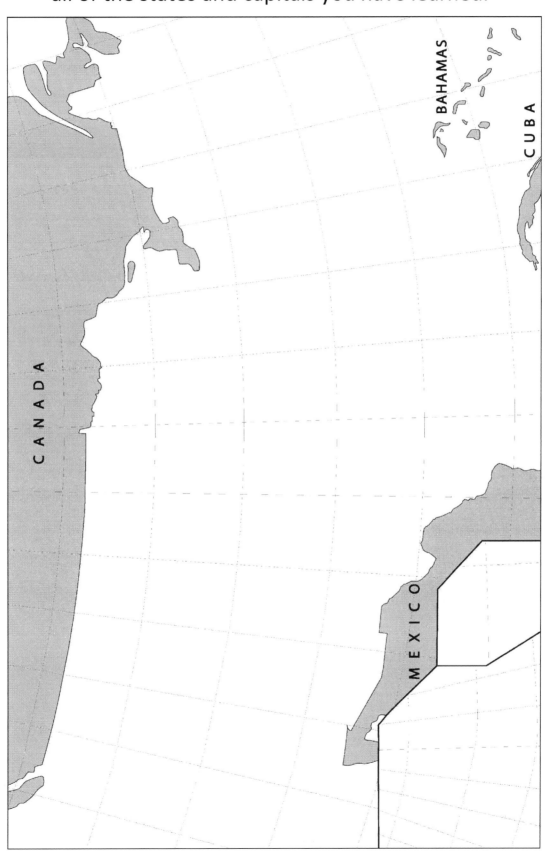

**Day 3:** On the map below, trace and label
all of the states and capitals you have learned.

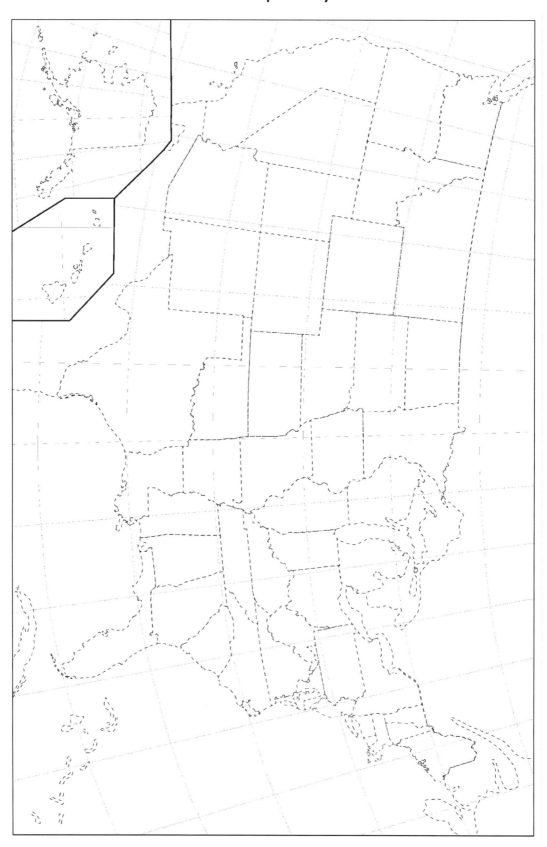

**Day 3:** On the map below, draw and label
all of the states and capitals you have learned.

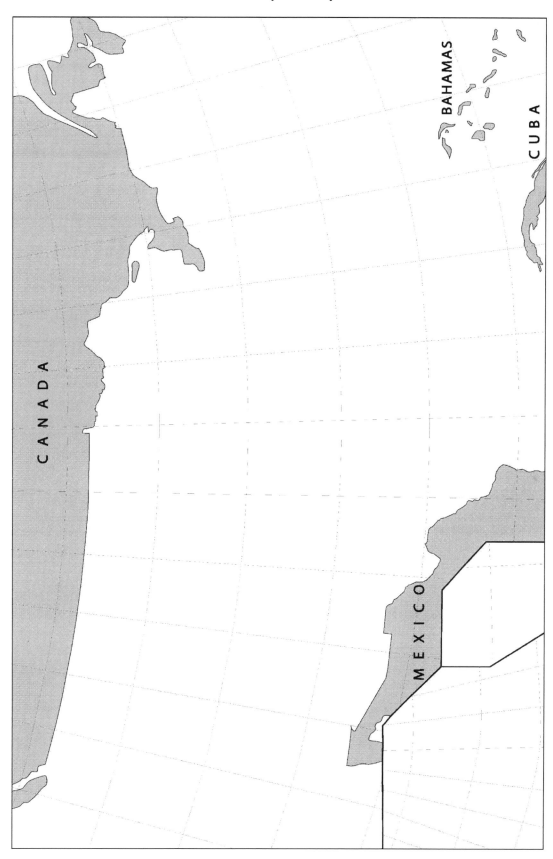

**Day 4:** On the lines below, list all of the states you have learned. On the small line, write the state abbreviation.

_____   _____

**Day 4:** On the map below, draw and label all of the states and capitals you have learned. Draw them without looking back.

# New Hampshire

Trace the state.
Draw it in the box below.

## State Facts

| | |
|---|---|
| Capital/Abbreviation | / |
| Area/Population | / |
| Statehood | |
| Bird/Flower | / |
| Industry | |
| Interesting Fact | |

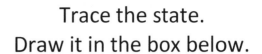

Trace the state.
Draw it in the box below.

Montpelier

## State Facts

| | |
|---|---|
| Capital/Abbreviation | / |
| Area/Population | / |
| Statehood | |
| Bird/Flower | / |
| Industry | |
| Interesting Fact | |

**Day 1:** On the map below, trace and label
the new state and capital (or states and capitals) you have learned.

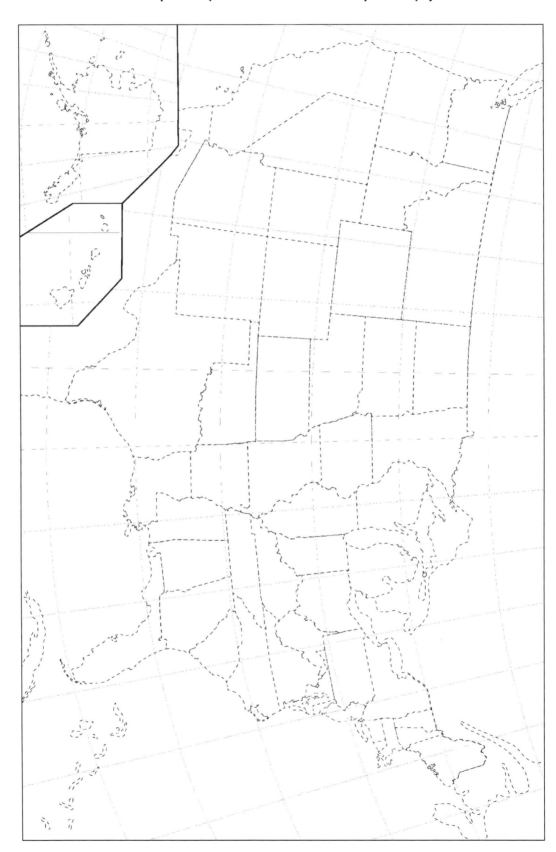

**Day 1:** On the map below, draw and label
the new state (or states) you have learned. Add the capital(s).

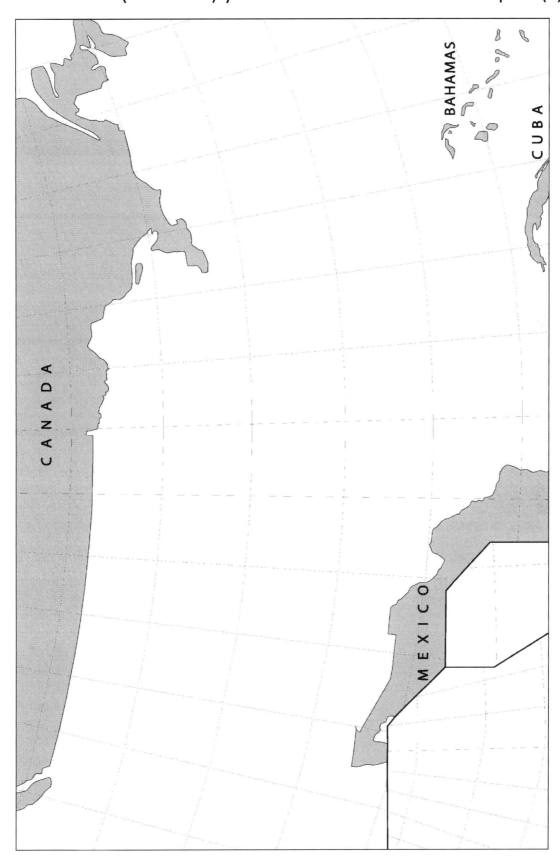

**Day 2:** On the map below, trace and label
all of the states and capitals you have learned.

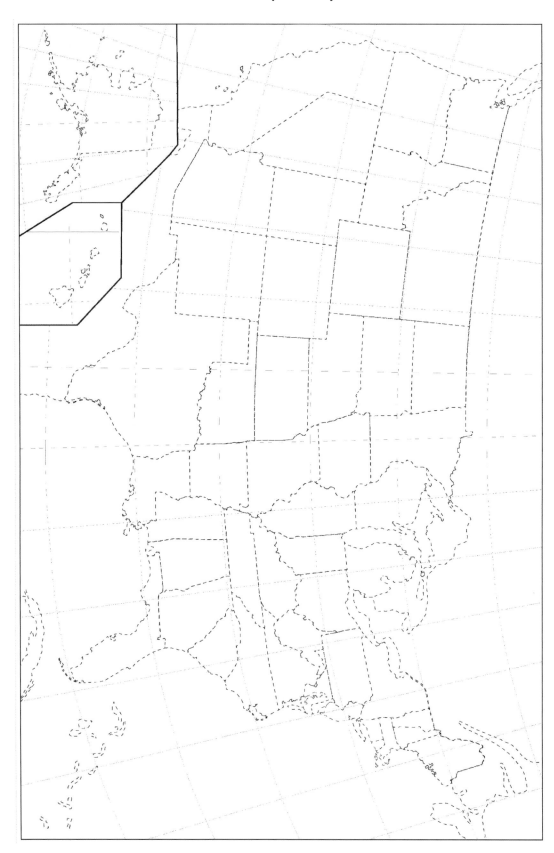

**Day 2:** On the map below, draw and label
all of the states and capitals you have learned.

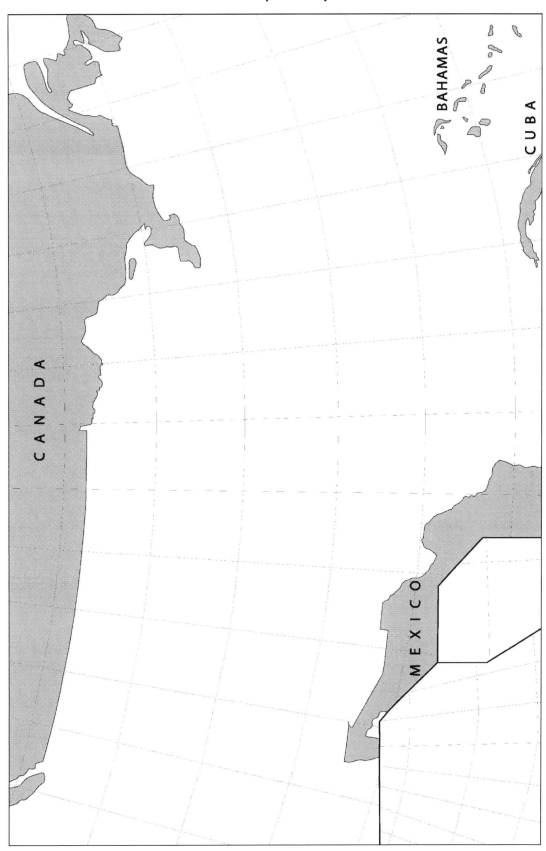

**Day 3:** On the map below, trace and label
all of the states and capitals you have learned.

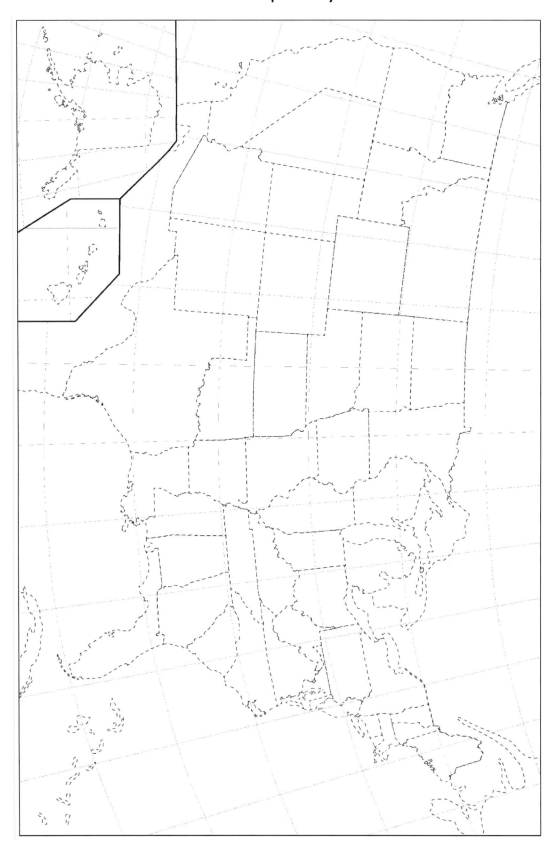

**Day 3:** On the map below, draw and label
all of the states and capitals you have learned.

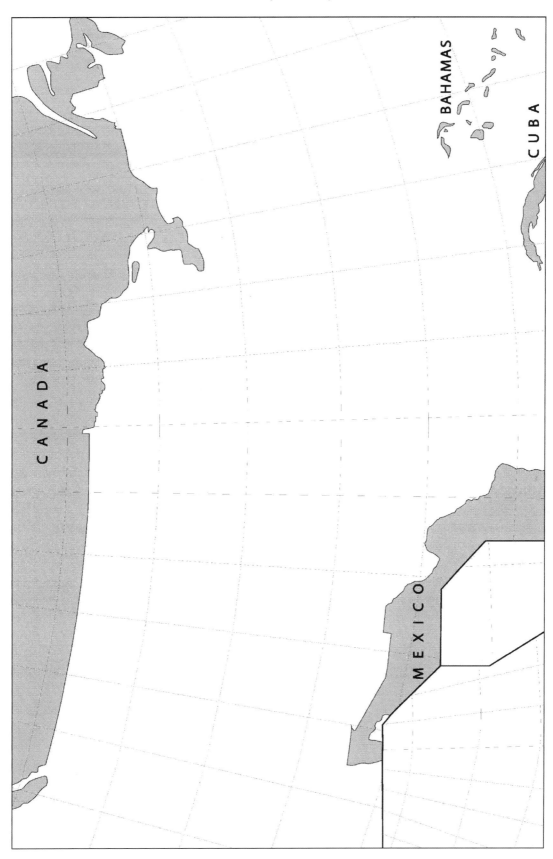

**Day 4:** On the lines below, list all of the states you have learned. On the small line, write the state abbreviation.

_____  _____

_____  _____

_____  _____

**Day 4:** On the map below, draw and label all of the states and capitals you have learned. Draw them without looking back.

# Massachusetts

Trace the state.
Draw it in the box below.

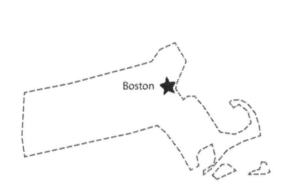

## State Facts

| | |
|---|---|
| Capital/Abbreviation | / |
| Area/Population | / |
| Statehood | |
| Bird/Flower | / |
| Industry | |
| Interesting Fact | |

# Rhode Island

Trace the state.
Draw it in the box below.

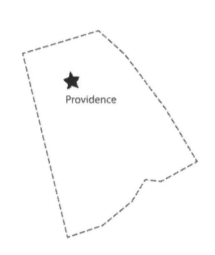

## State Facts

| | |
|---|---|
| Capital/Abbreviation | / |
| Area/Population | / |
| Statehood | |
| Bird/Flower | / |
| Industry | |
| Interesting Fact | |

# Connecticut

Trace the state.
Draw it in the box below.

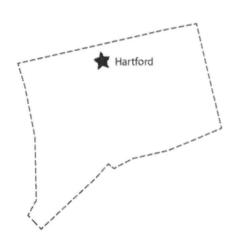

## State Facts

| | |
|---|---|
| Capital/Abbreviation | / |
| Area/Population | / |
| Statehood | |
| Bird/Flower | / |
| Industry | |
| Interesting Fact | |

**Day 1:** On the map below, trace and label
the new state and capital (or states and capitals) you have learned.

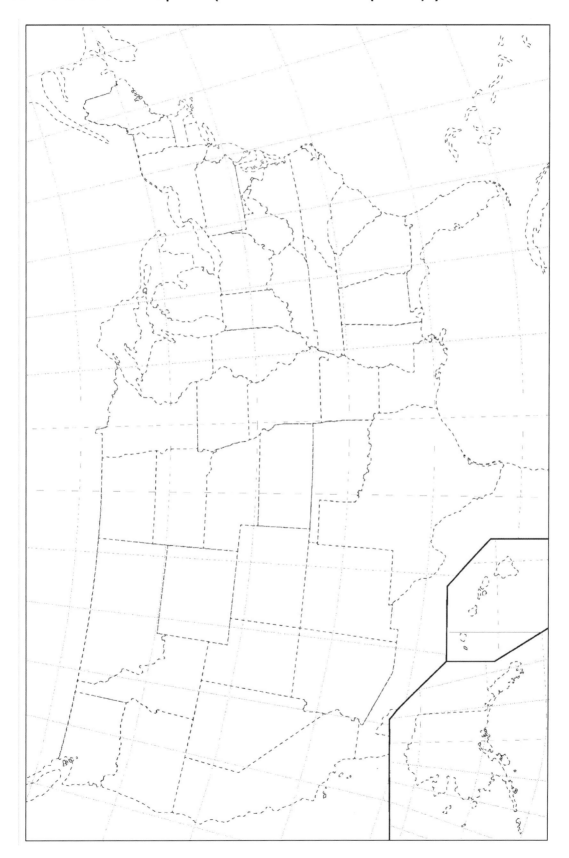

**Day 1:** On the map below, draw and label
the new state (or states) you have learned. Add the capital(s).

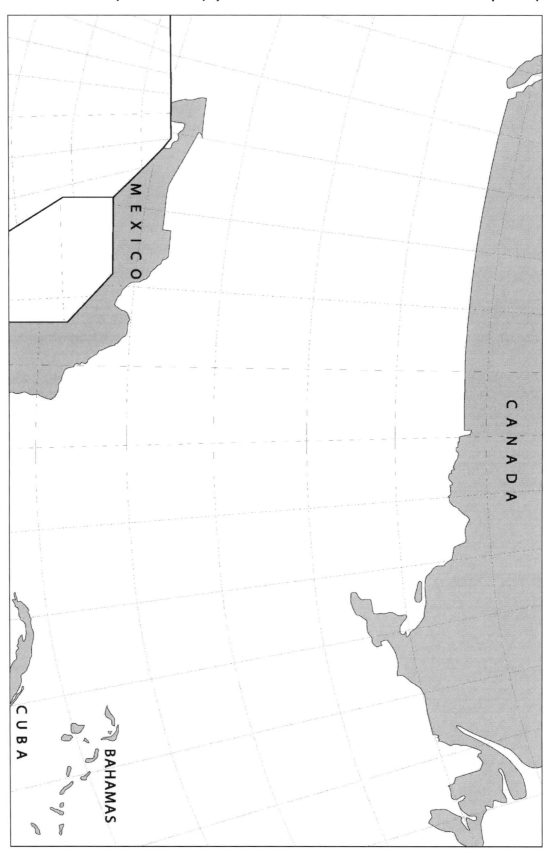

**Day 2:** On the map below, trace and label
all of the states and capitals you have learned.

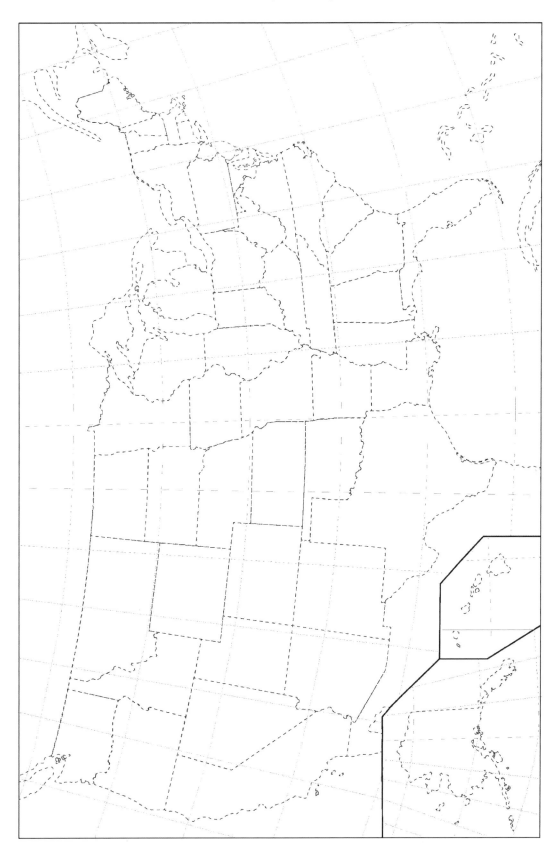

**Day 2:** On the map below, draw and label all of the states and capitals you have learned.

**Day 3:** On the map below, trace and label
all of the states and capitals you have learned.

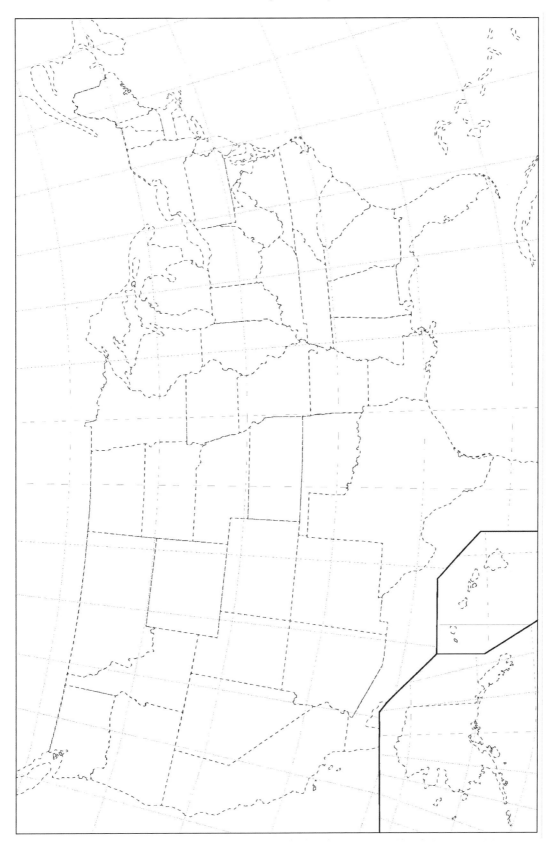

**Day 3:** On the map below, draw and label
all of the states and capitals you have learned.

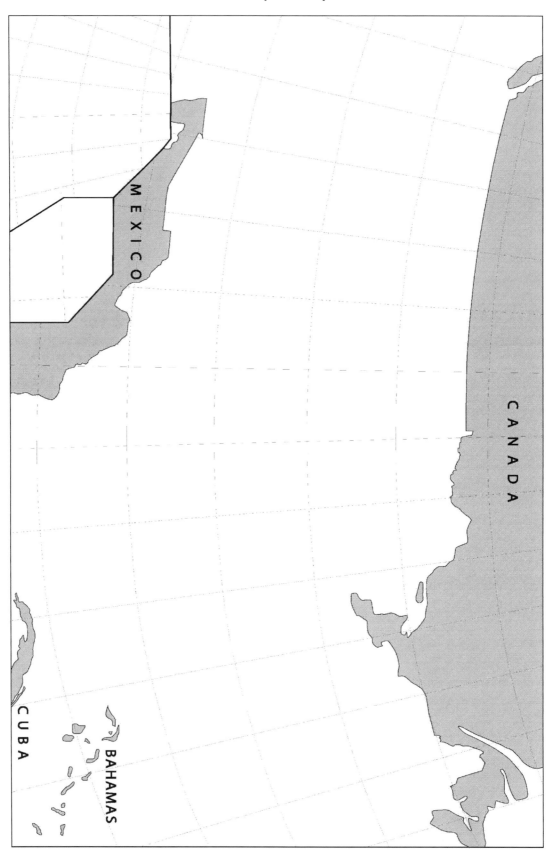

**Day 4:** On the lines below, list all of the states you have learned. On the small line, write the state abbreviation.

_____  _____        _____  _____

_____  _____        _____  _____

_____  _____

_____  _____

**Day 4:** On the map below, draw and label all of the states and capitals you have learned. Draw them without looking back.

# New York

Trace the state.
Draw it in the box below.

Albany

## State Facts

| Capital/Abbreviation | / |
| --- | --- |
| Area/Population | / |
| Statehood | |
| Bird/Flower | / |
| Industry | |
| Interesting Fact | |

**Day 1:** On the map below, trace and label
the new state and capital (or states and capitals) you have learned.

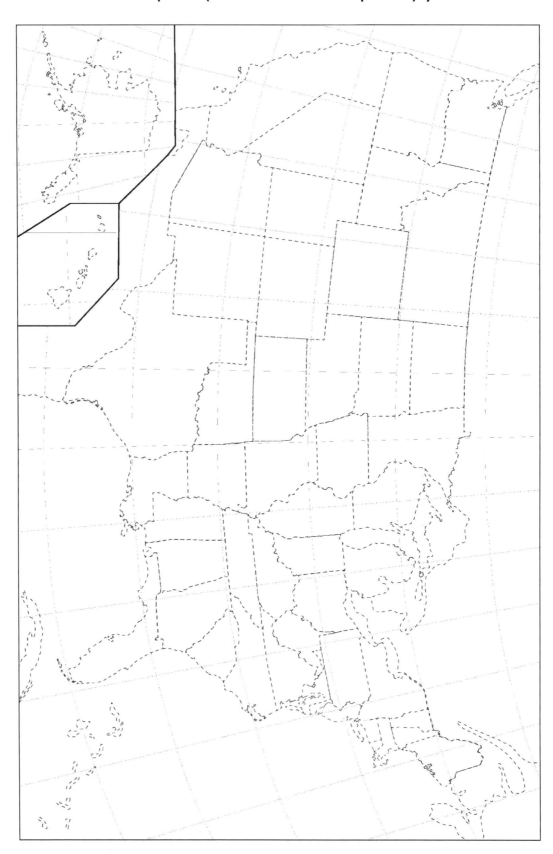

**Day 1:** On the map below, draw and label
the new state (or states) you have learned. Add the capital(s).

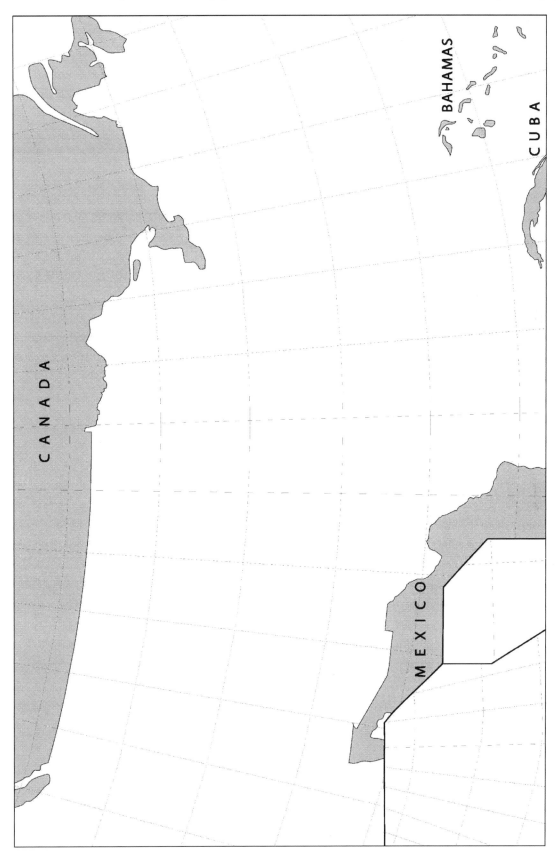

**Day 2:** On the map below, trace and label
all of the states and capitals you have learned.

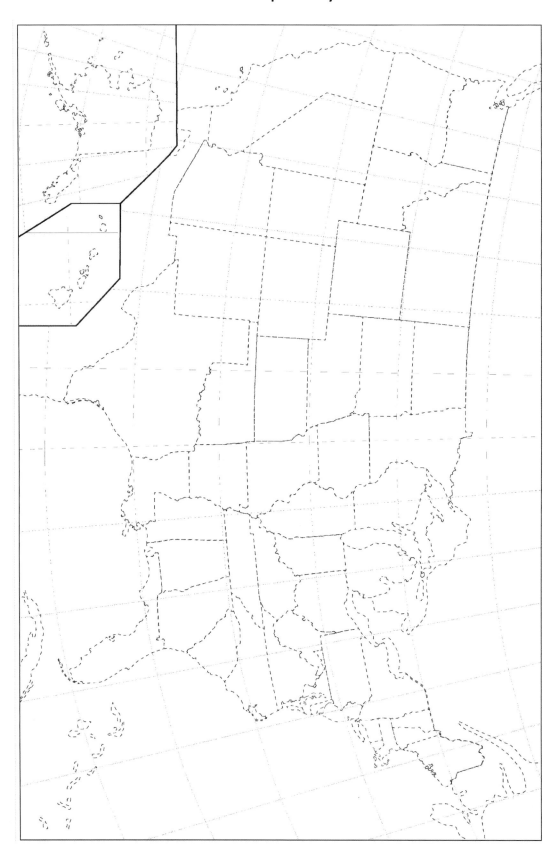

**Day 2:** On the map below, draw and label
all of the states and capitals you have learned.

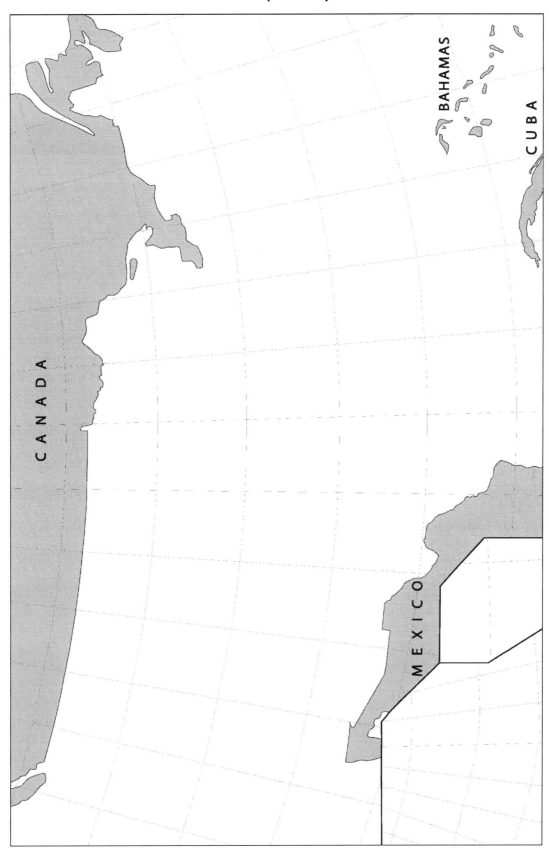

**Day 3:** On the map below, trace and label
all of the states and capitals you have learned.

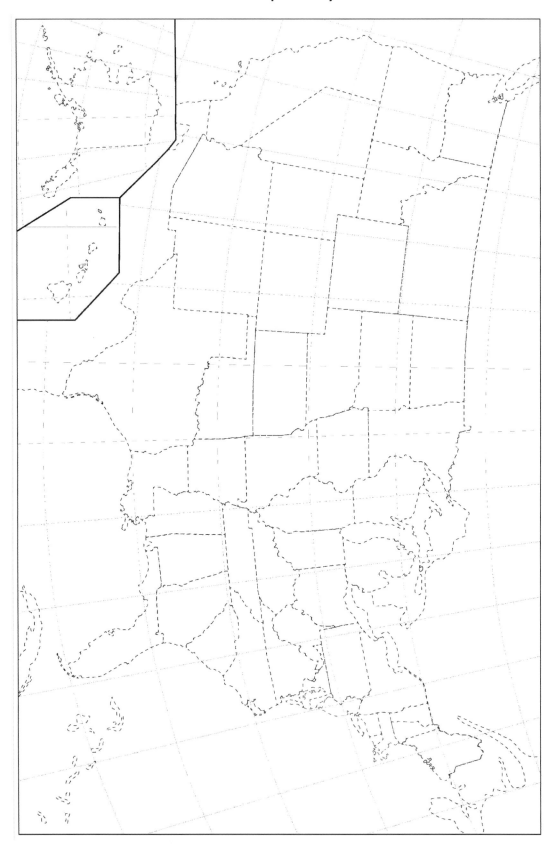

**Day 3:** On the map below, draw and label
all of the states and capitals you have learned.

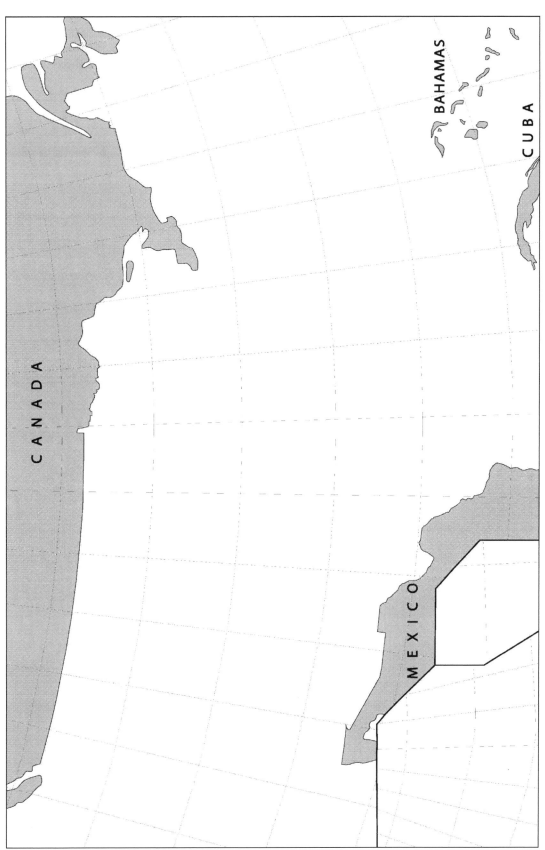

**Day 4:** On the lines below, list all of the states you have learned. On the small line, write the state abbreviation.

_____  _____          _____  _____

_____  _____          _____  _____

_____  _____          _____  _____

_____  _____

**Day 4:** On the map below, draw and label all of the states and capitals you have learned. Draw them without looking back.

# Pennsylvania

Trace the state.
Draw it in the box below.

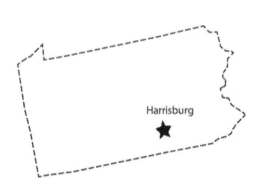

## State Facts

| | |
|---|---|
| Capital/Abbreviation | / |
| Area/Population | / |
| Statehood | |
| Bird/Flower | / |
| Industry | |
| Interesting Fact | |

**Day 1:** On the map below, trace and label
the new state and capital (or states and capitals) you have learned.

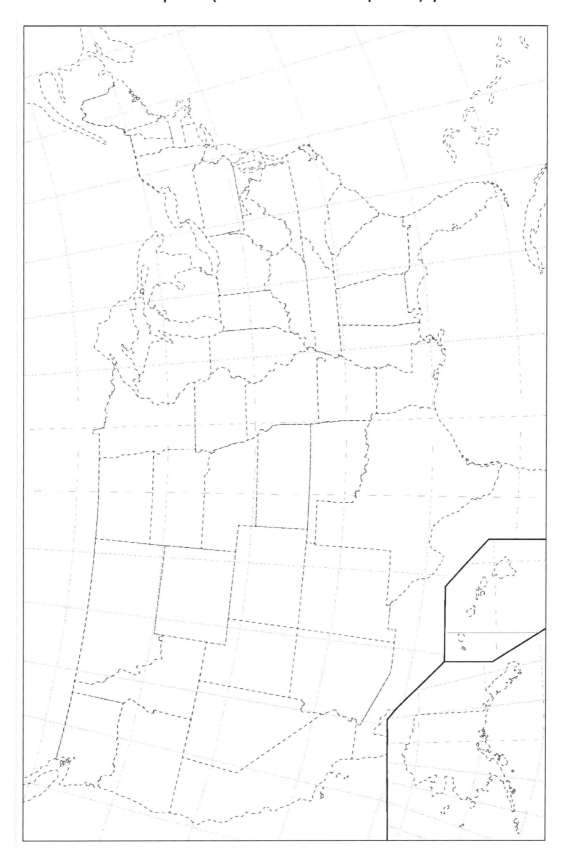

**Day 1:** On the map below, draw and label
the new state (or states) you have learned. Add the capital(s).

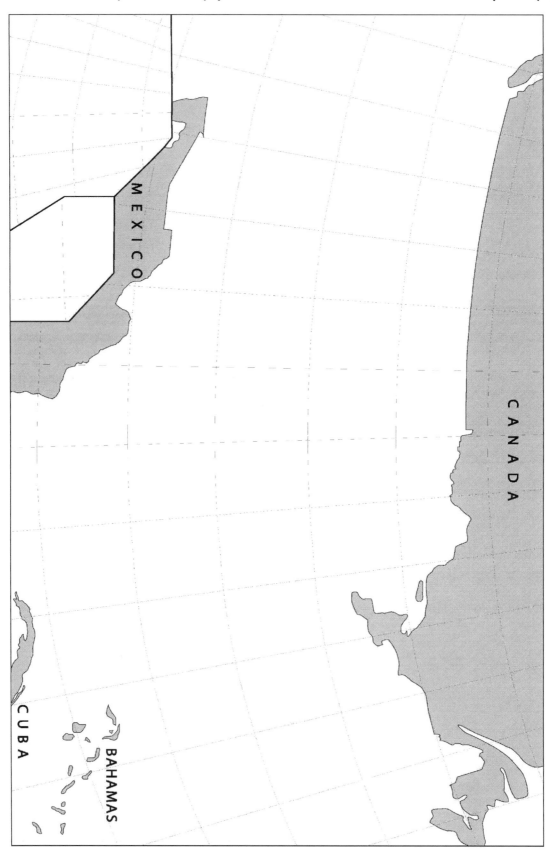

**Day 2:** On the map below, trace and label
all of the states and capitals you have learned.

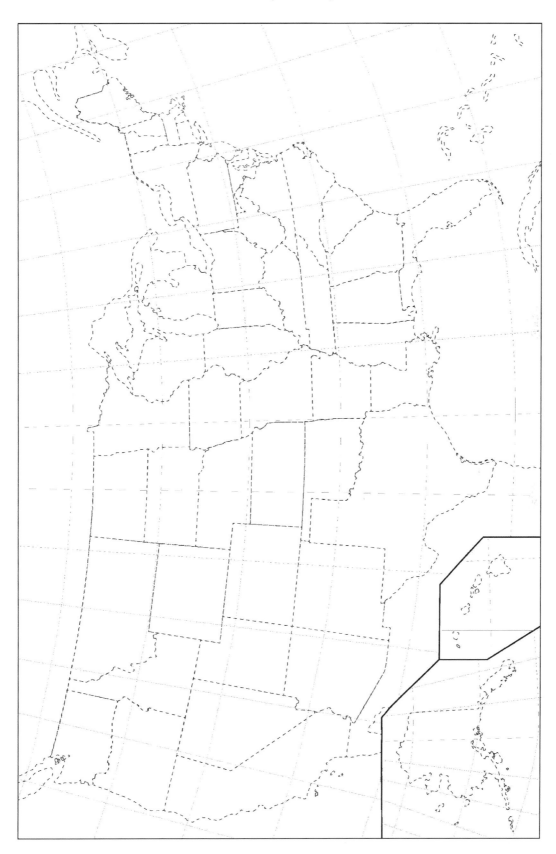

**Day 2:** On the map below, draw and label all of the states and capitals you have learned.

**Day 3:** On the map below, trace and label
all of the states and capitals you have learned.

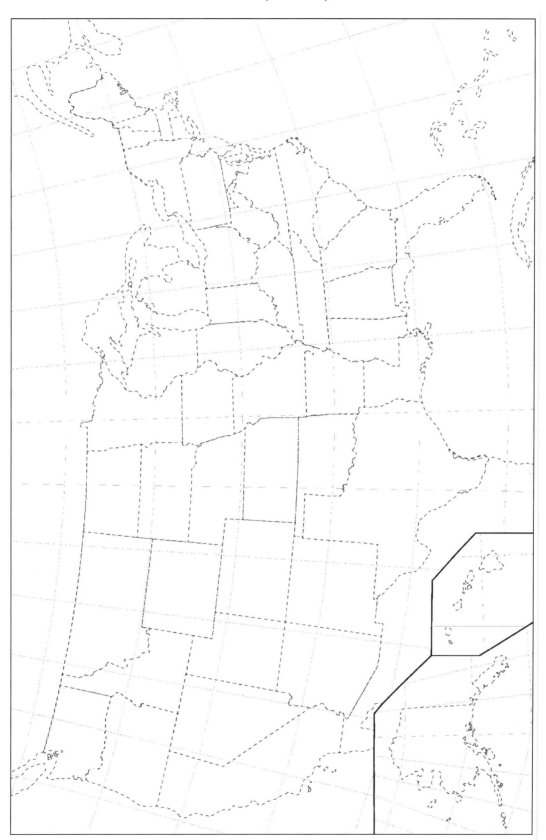

**Day 3:** On the map below, draw and label
all of the states and capitals you have learned.

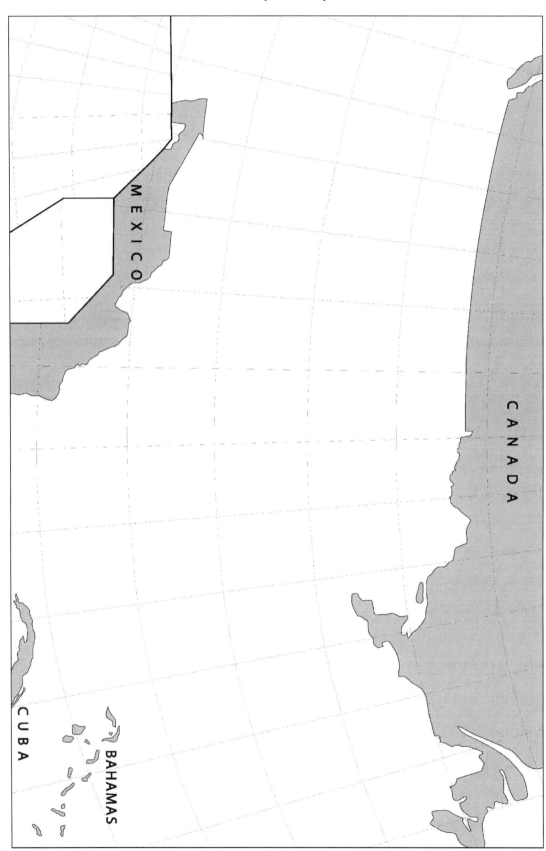

**Day 4:** On the lines below, list all of the states you have learned. On the small line, write the state abbreviation.

_____  _____        _____  _____

_____  _____        _____  _____

_____  _____        _____  _____

_____  _____

_____  _____

**Day 4:** On the map below, draw and label all of the states and capitals you have learned. Draw them without looking back.

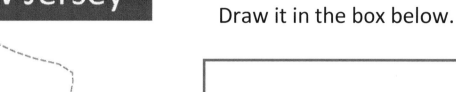

Trace the state.
Draw it in the box below.

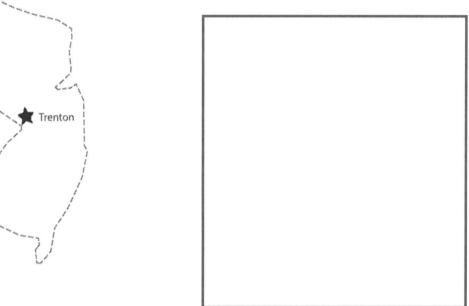

## State Facts

| Capital/Abbreviation | / |
|---|---|
| Area/Population | / |
| Statehood | |
| Bird/Flower | / |
| Industry | |
| Interesting Fact | |

**Day 1:** On the map below, trace and label the new state and capital (or states and capitals) you have learned.

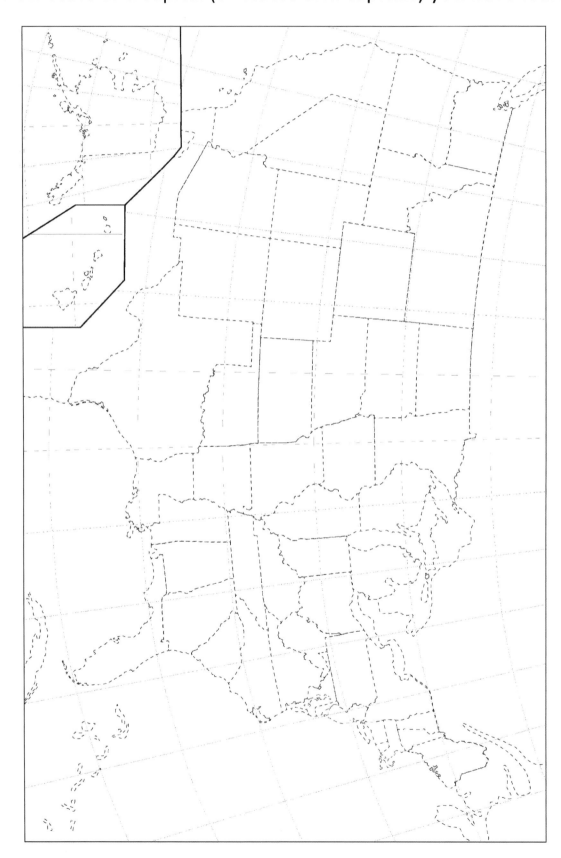

**Day 1:** On the map below, draw and label
the new state (or states) you have learned. Add the capital(s).

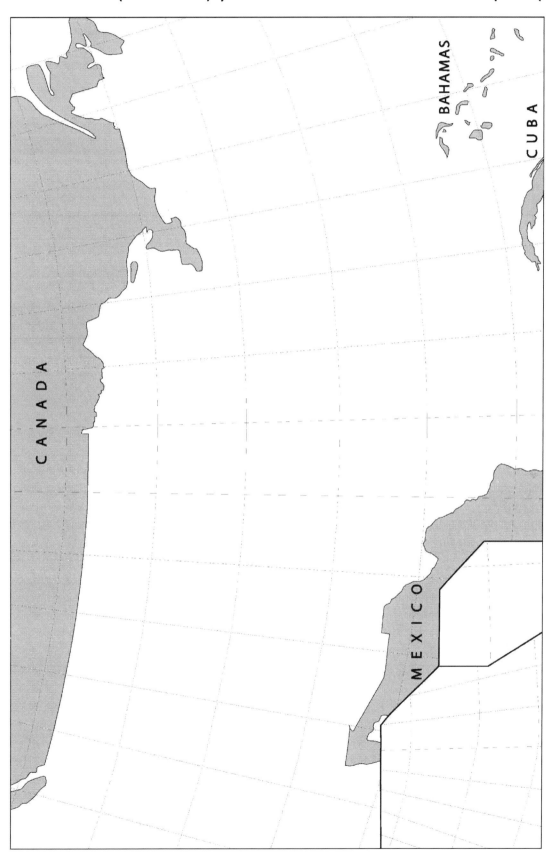

**Day 2:** On the map below, trace and label
all of the states and capitals you have learned.

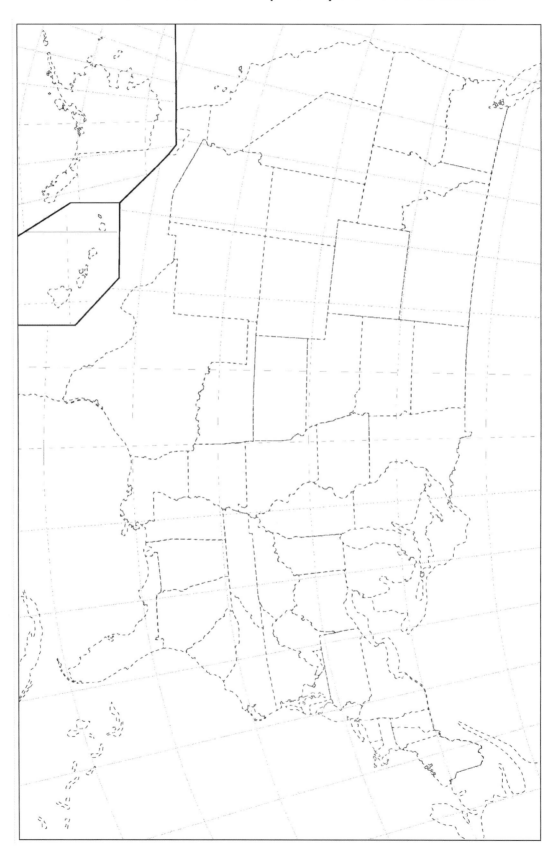

**Day 2:** On the map below, draw and label
all of the states and capitals you have learned.

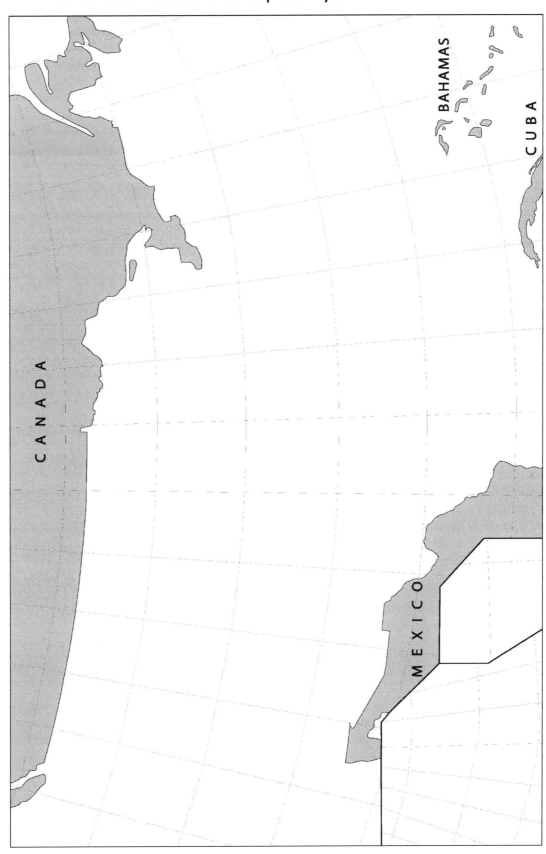

**Day 3:** On the map below, trace and label
all of the states and capitals you have learned.

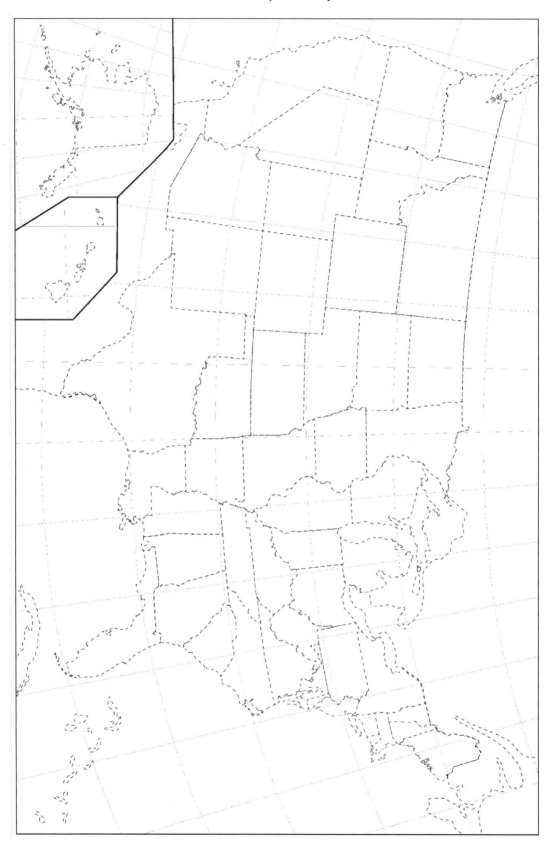

**Day 3:** On the map below, draw and label
all of the states and capitals you have learned.

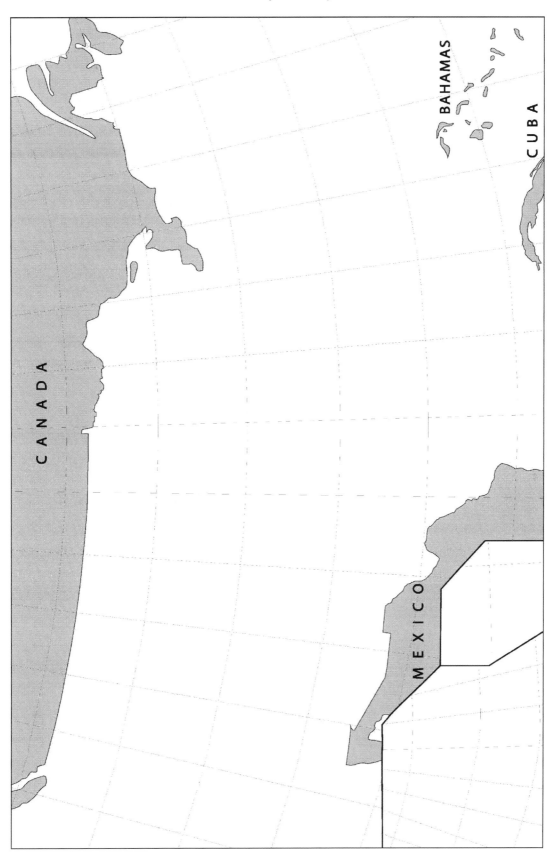

**Day 4:** On the lines below, list all of the states you have learned. On the small line, write the state abbreviation.

_____   _____

_____   _____

_____   _____

_____   _____

_____   _____

_____   _____

_____   _____

_____   _____

_____   _____

**Day 4:** On the map below, draw and label all of the states and capitals you have learned. Draw them without looking back.

# Delaware

Trace the state.
Draw it in the box below.

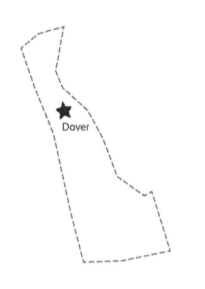

## State Facts

| | |
|---|---|
| Capital/Abbreviation | / |
| Area/Population | / |
| Statehood | |
| Bird/Flower | / |
| Industry | |
| Interesting Fact | |

# Maryland

Trace the state.
Draw it in the box below.

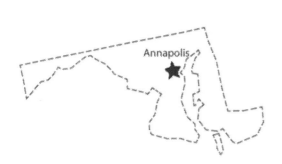

## State Facts

| | |
|---|---|
| Capital/Abbreviation | / |
| Area/Population | / |
| Statehood | |
| Bird/Flower | / |
| Industry | |
| Interesting Fact | |

## Washington D. C.

Trace the state.
Draw it in the box below.

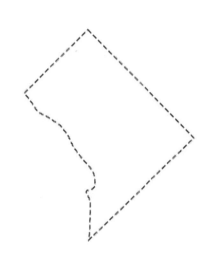

## State Facts

| | |
|---|---|
| Capital/Abbreviation | / |
| Area/Population | / |
| Statehood | |
| Bird/Flower | / |
| Industry | |
| Interesting Fact | |

**Day 1:** On the map below, trace and label
the new state and capital (or states and capitals) you have learned.

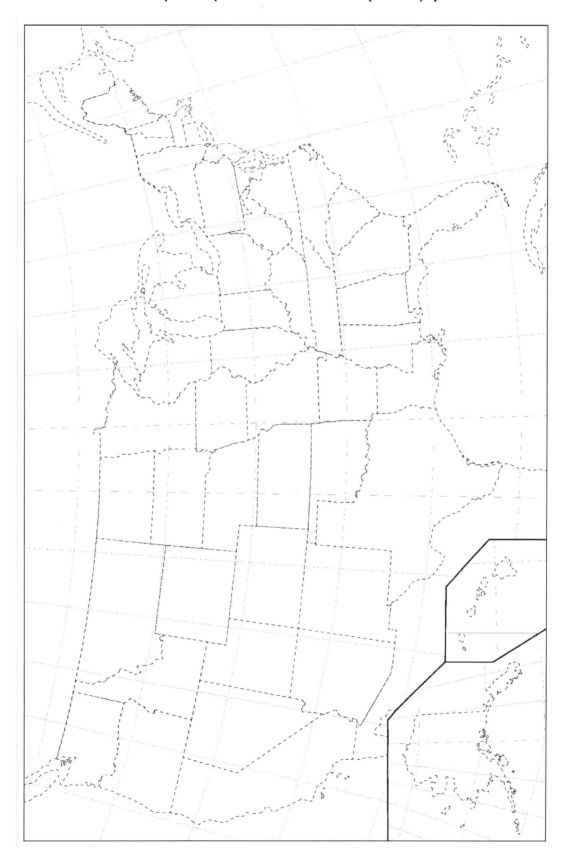

**Day 1:** On the map below, draw and label
the new state (or states) you have learned. Add the capital(s).

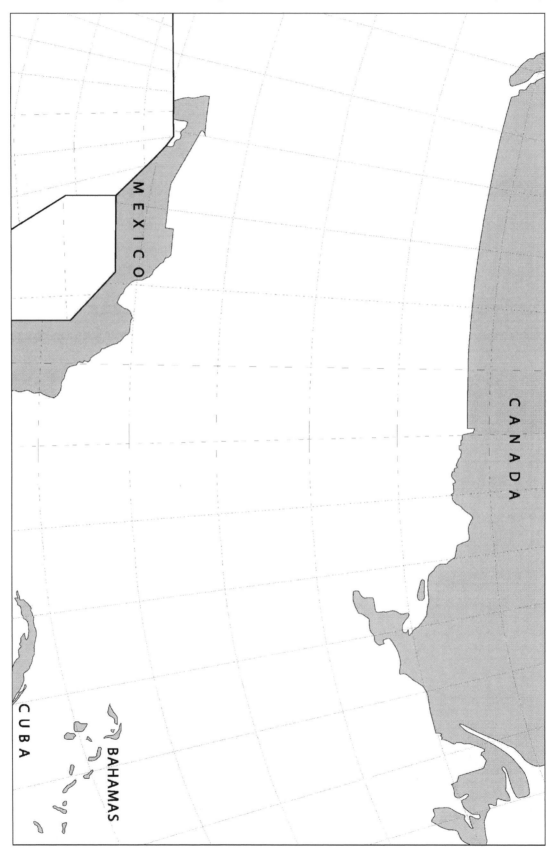

**Day 2:** On the map below, trace and label
all of the states and capitals you have learned.

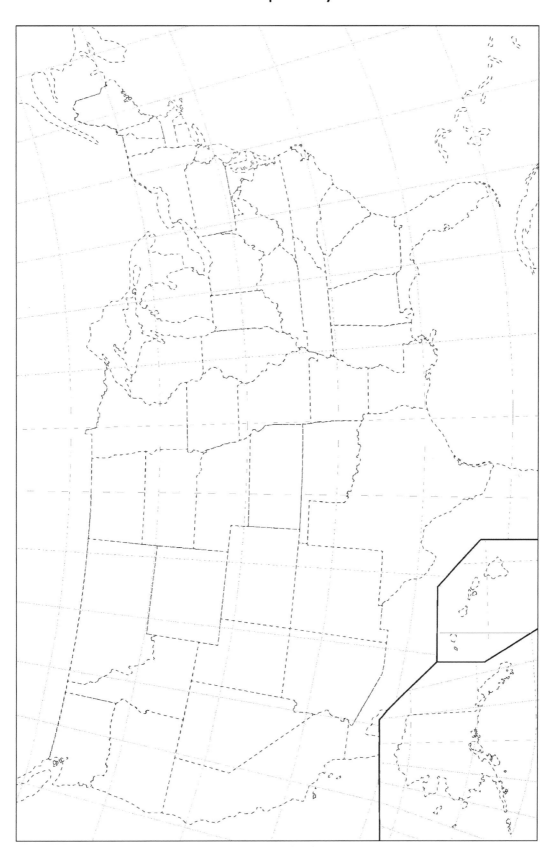

**Day 2:** On the map below, draw and label
all of the states and capitals you have learned.

**Day 3:** On the map below, trace and label
all of the states and capitals you have learned.

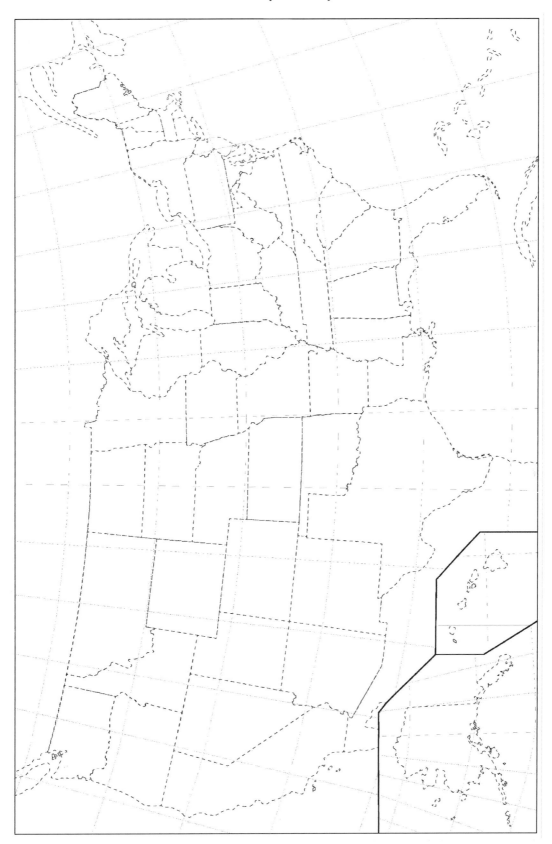

**Day 3:** On the map below, draw and label
all of the states and capitals you have learned.

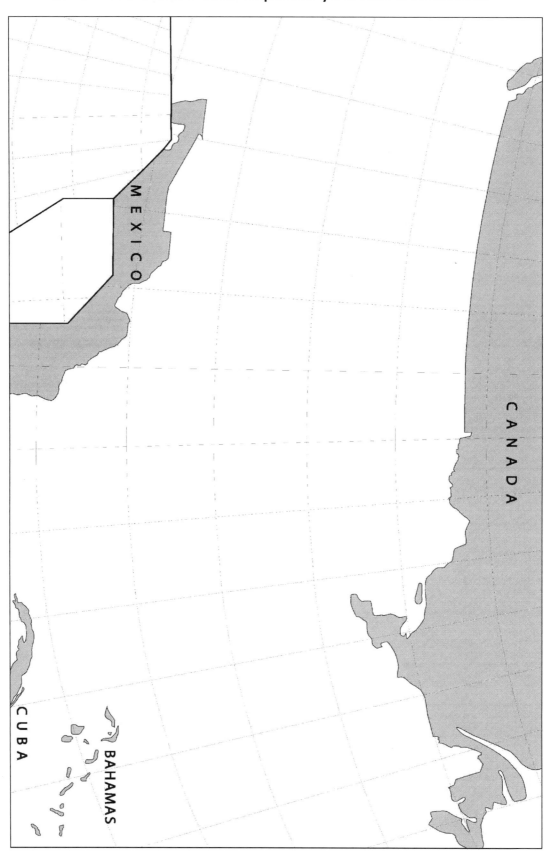

**Day 4:** On the lines below, list all of the states you have learned. On the small line, write the state abbreviation.

_____  _____

_____  _____

_____  _____

_____  _____

_____  _____

_____  _____

_____  _____

_____  _____

_____  _____

_____  _____

_____  _____

_____  _____

**Day 4:** On the map below, draw and label all of the states and capitals you have learned. Draw them without looking back.

# West Virginia

Trace the state.
Draw it in the box below.

## State Facts

| | |
|---|---|
| Capital/Abbreviation | / |
| Area/Population | / |
| Statehood | |
| Bird/Flower | / |
| Industry | |
| Interesting Fact | |

# Virginia

Trace the state.
Draw it in the box below.

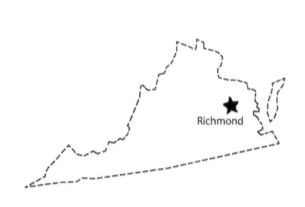

## State Facts

| | |
|---|---|
| Capital/Abbreviation | / |
| Area/Population | / |
| Statehood | |
| Bird/Flower | / |
| Industry | |
| Interesting Fact | |

**Day 1:** On the map below, trace and label
the new state and capital (or states and capitals) you have learned.

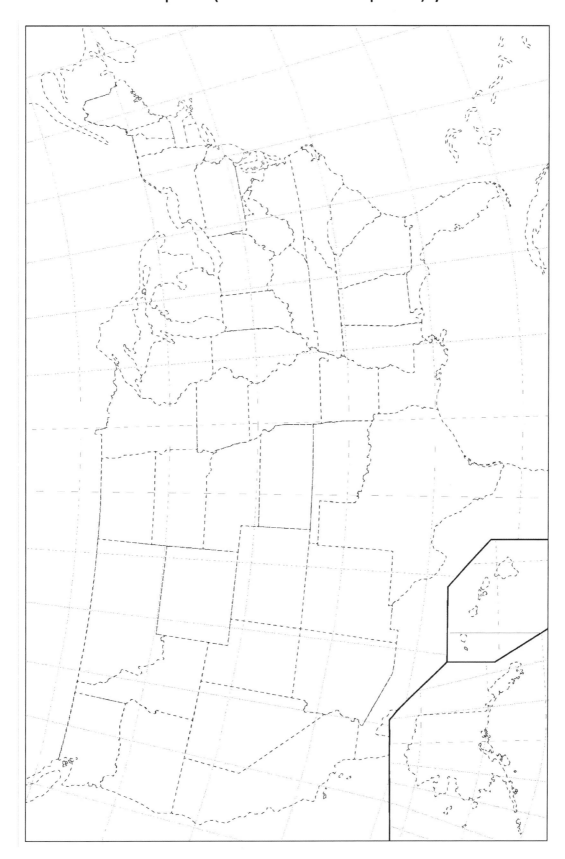

**Day 1:** On the map below, draw and label
the new state (or states) you have learned. Add the capital(s).

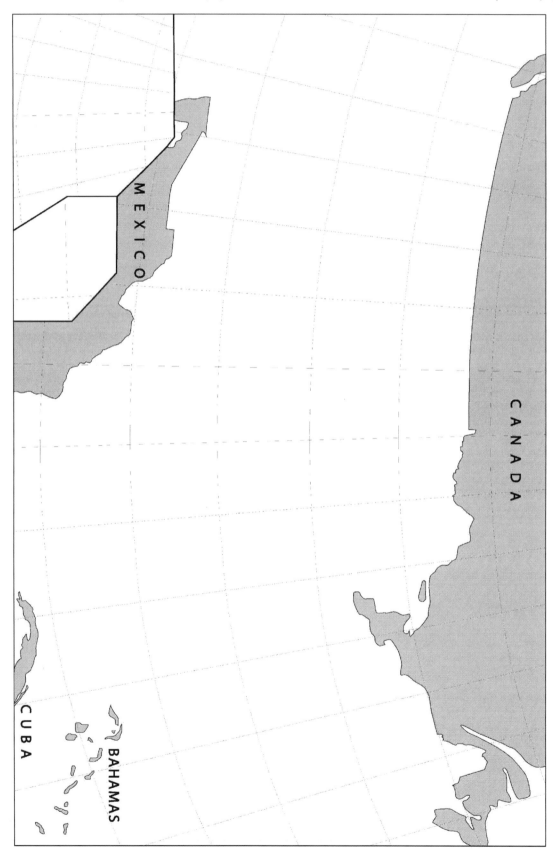

**Day 2:** On the map below, trace and label
all of the states and capitals you have learned.

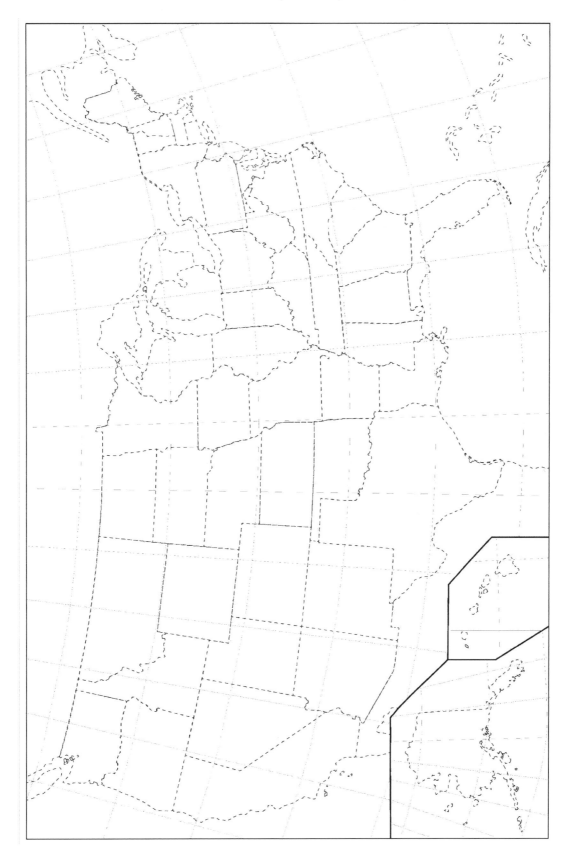

**Day 2:** On the map below, draw and label
all of the states and capitals you have learned.

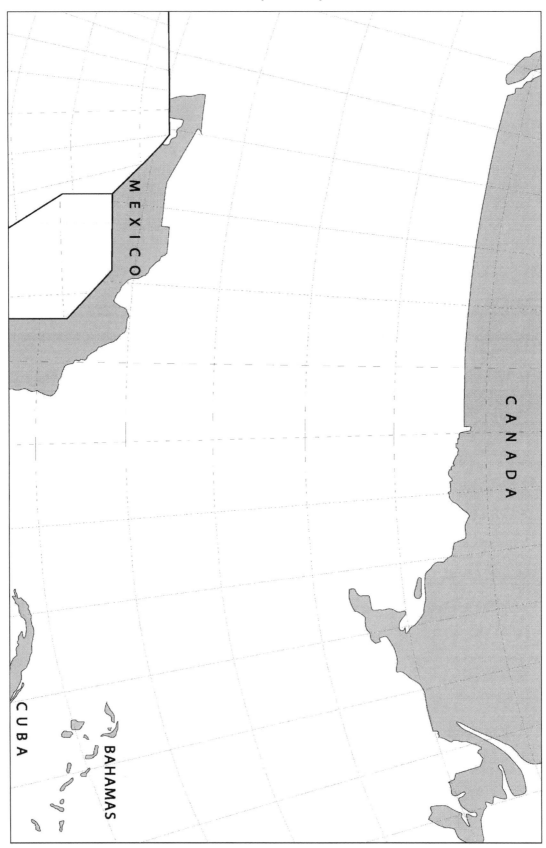

**Day 3:** On the map below, trace and label
all of the states and capitals you have learned.

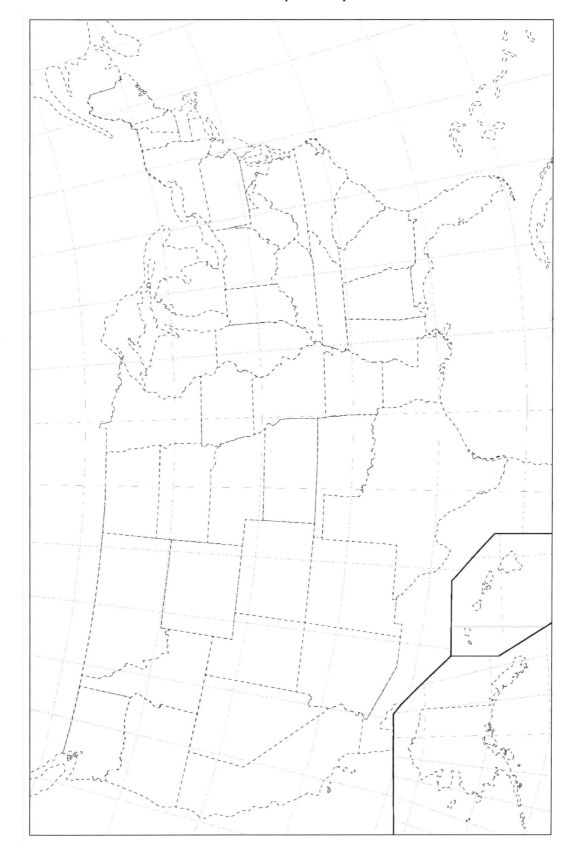

**Day 3:** On the map below, draw and label all of the states and capitals you have learned.

**Day 4:** On the lines below, list all of the states you have learned. On the small line, write the state abbreviation.

**Day 4:** On the map below, draw and label all of the states and capitals you have learned. Draw them without looking back.

# North Carolina

Trace the state.
Draw it in the box below.

## State Facts

| Capital/Abbreviation | / |
|---|---|
| Area/Population | / |
| Statehood | |
| Bird/Flower | / |
| Industry | |
| Interesting Fact | |

# South Carolina

Trace the state.
Draw it in the box below.

## State Facts

| | |
|---|---|
| Capital/Abbreviation | / |
| Area/Population | / |
| Statehood | |
| Bird/Flower | / |
| Industry | |
| Interesting Fact | |

**Day 1:** On the map below, trace and label
the new state and capital (or states and capitals) you have learned.

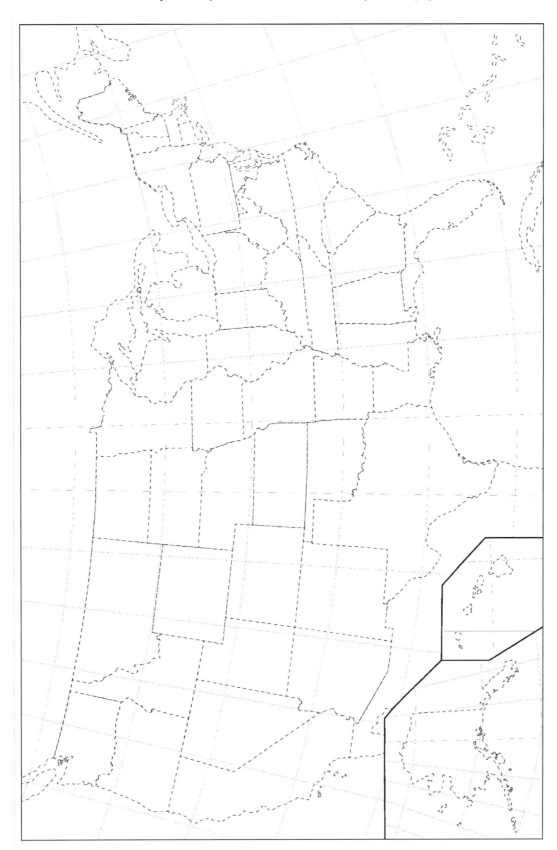

**Day 1:** On the map below, draw and label
the new state (or states) you have learned. Add the capital(s).

**Day 2:** On the map below, trace and label
all of the states and capitals you have learned.

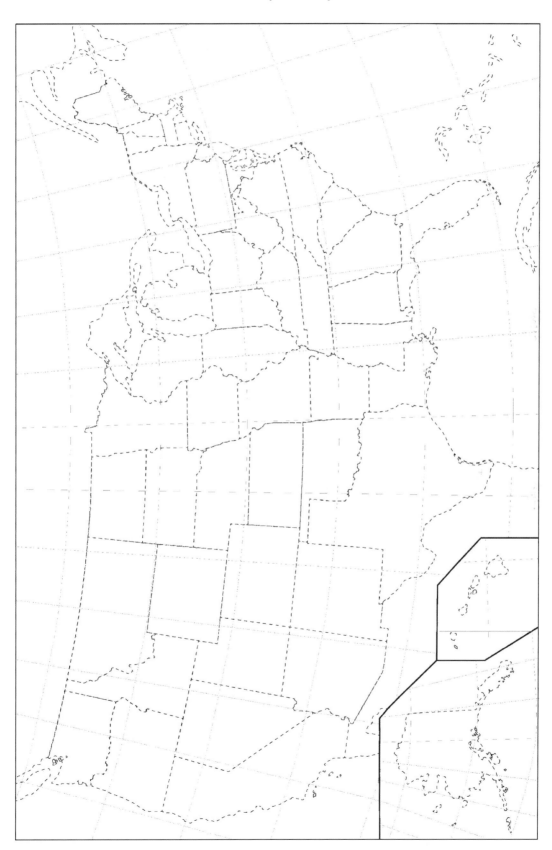

**Day 2:** On the map below, draw and label
all of the states and capitals you have learned.

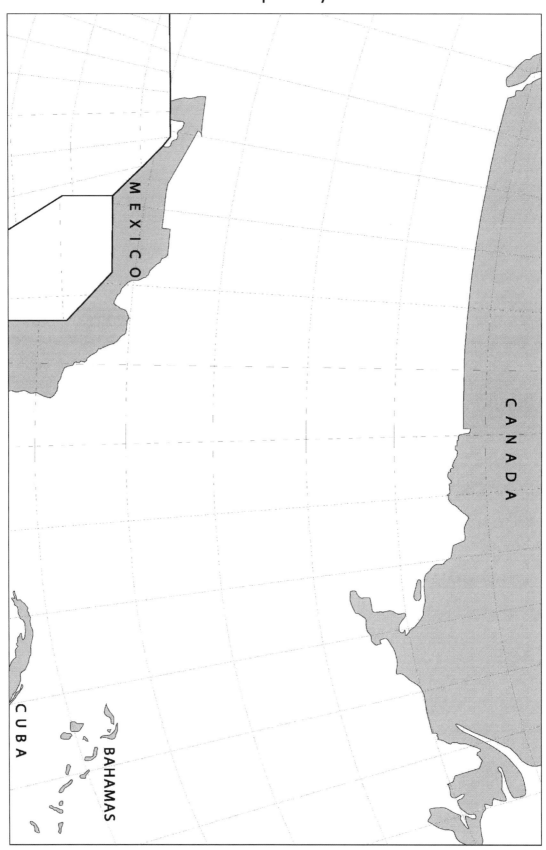

**Day 3:** On the map below, trace and label
all of the states and capitals you have learned.

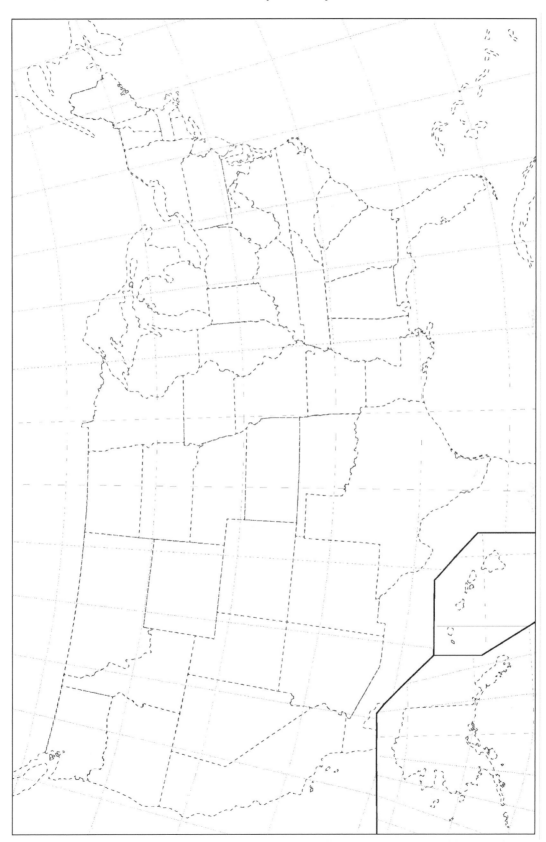

**Day 3:** On the map below, draw and label
all of the states and capitals you have learned.

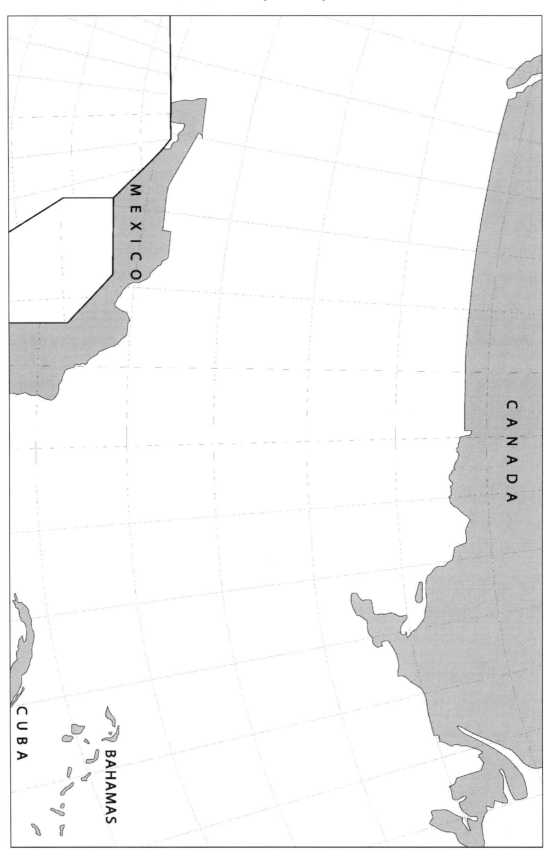

**Day 4:** On the lines below, list all of the states you have learned. On the small line, write the state abbreviation.

_____ _____

_____ _____

_____ _____

_____ _____

_____ _____

_____ _____

_____ _____

_____ _____

_____ _____

_____ _____

_____ _____

_____ _____

_____ _____

_____ _____

_____ _____

_____ _____

**Day 4:** On the map below, draw and label all of the states and capitals you have learned. Draw them without looking back.

# Georgia

Trace the state.
Draw it in the box below.

## State Facts

| | |
|---|---|
| Capital/Abbreviation | / |
| Area/Population | / |
| Statehood | |
| Bird/Flower | / |
| Industry | |
| Interesting Fact | |

**Day 1:** On the map below, trace and label
the new state and capital (or states and capitals) you have learned.

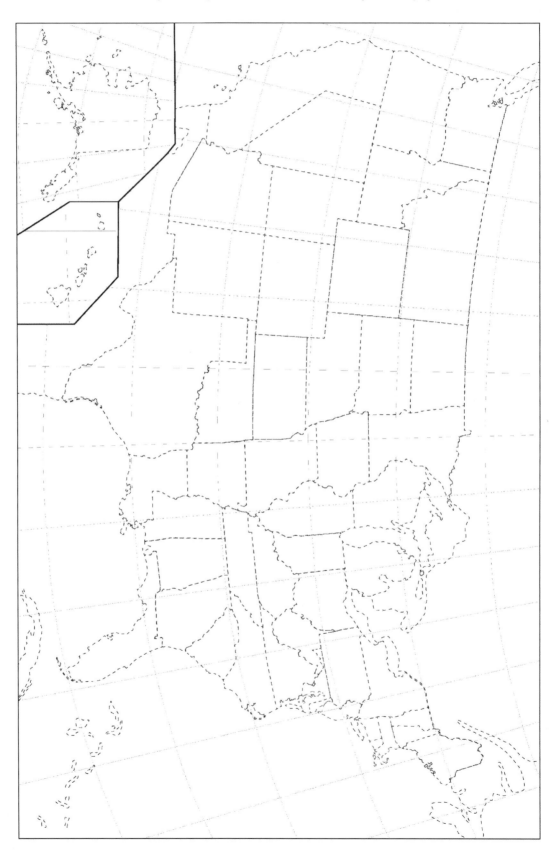

**Day 1:** On the map below, draw and label the new state (or states) you have learned. Add the capital(s).

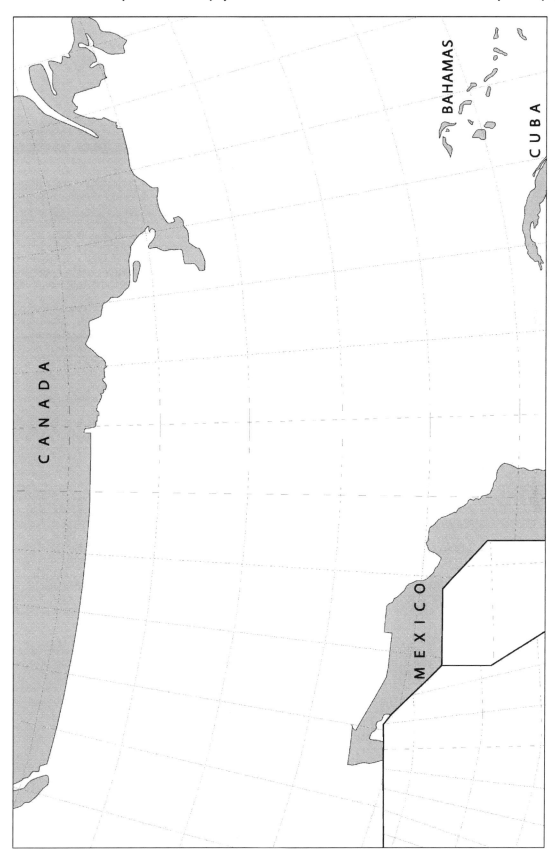

**Day 2:** On the map below, trace and label
all of the states and capitals you have learned.

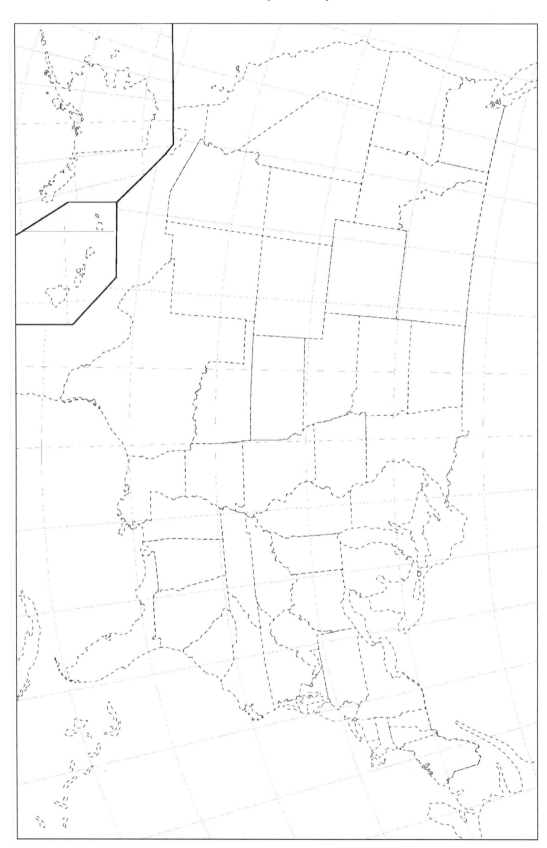

**Day 2:** On the map below, draw and label
all of the states and capitals you have learned.

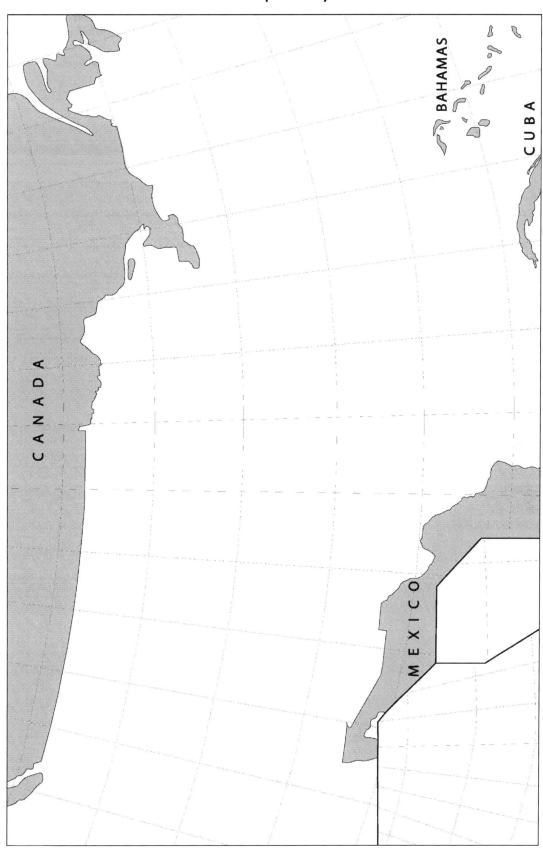

**Day 3:** On the map below, trace and label
all of the states and capitals you have learned.

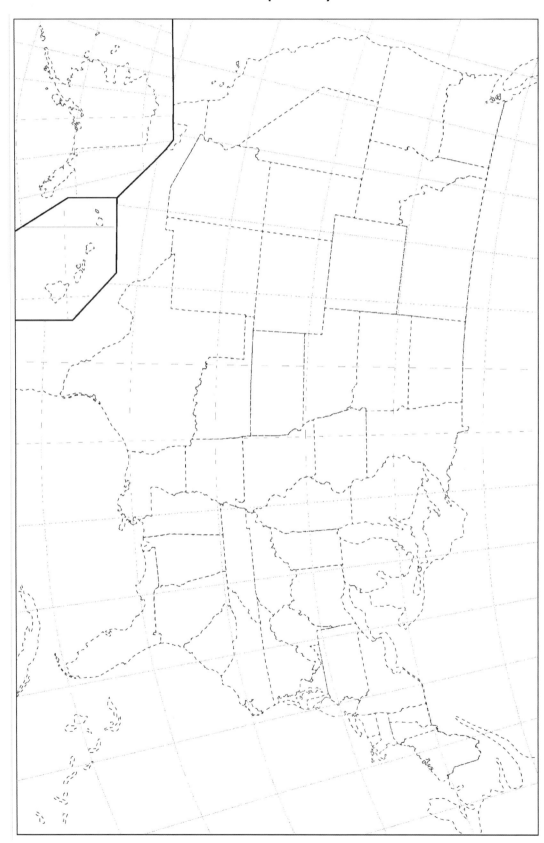

**Day 3:** On the map below, draw and label
all of the states and capitals you have learned.

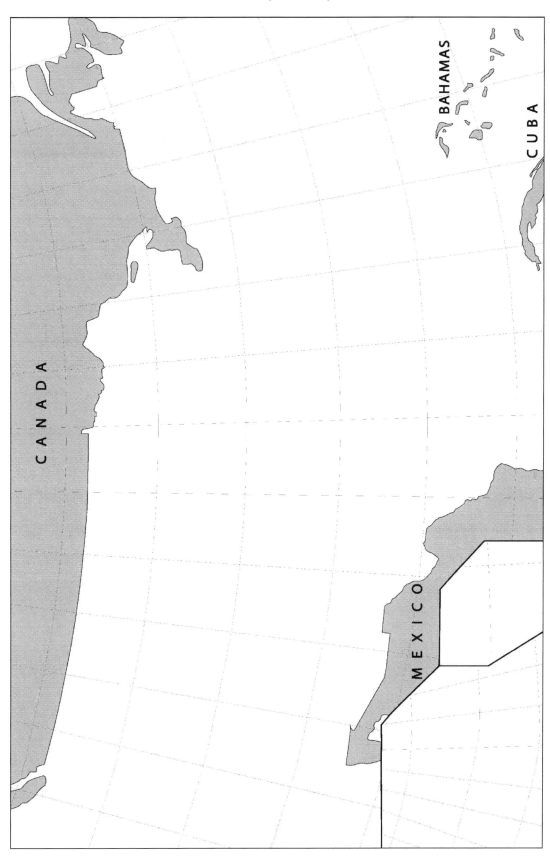

**Day 4:** On the lines below, list all of the states you have learned. On the small line, write the state abbreviation.

_____  _____    _____  _____

_____  _____    _____  _____

_____  _____    _____  _____

_____  _____    _____  _____

_____  _____    _____  _____

_____  _____    _____  _____

_____  _____    _____  _____

_____  _____    _____  _____

_____  _____

**Day 4:** On the map below, draw and label all of the states and capitals you have learned. Draw them without looking back.

# Florida

Trace the state.
Draw it in the box below.

## State Facts

| | |
|---|---|
| Capital/Abbreviation | / |
| Area/Population | / |
| Statehood | |
| Bird/Flower | / |
| Industry | |
| Interesting Fact | |

**Day 1:** On the map below, trace and label
the new state and capital (or states and capitals) you have learned.

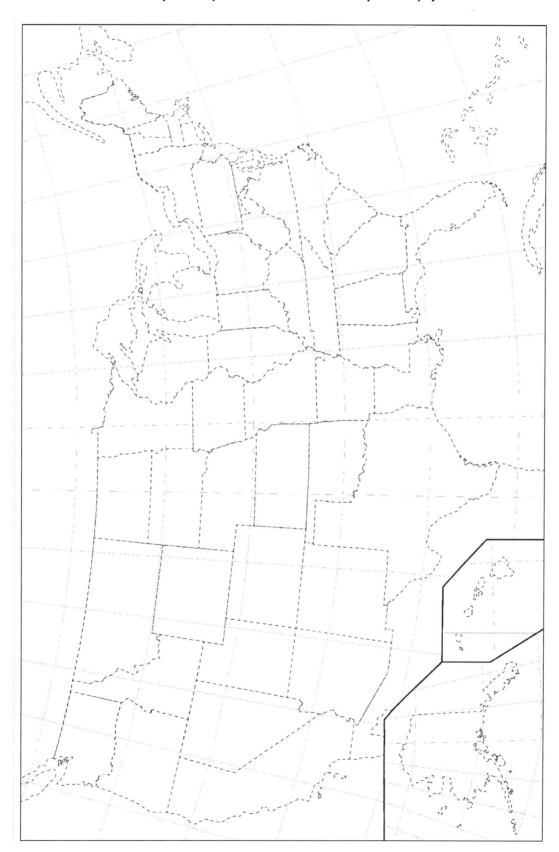

**Day 1:** On the map below, draw and label
the new state (or states) you have learned. Add the capital(s).

**Day 2:** On the map below, trace and label
all of the states and capitals you have learned.

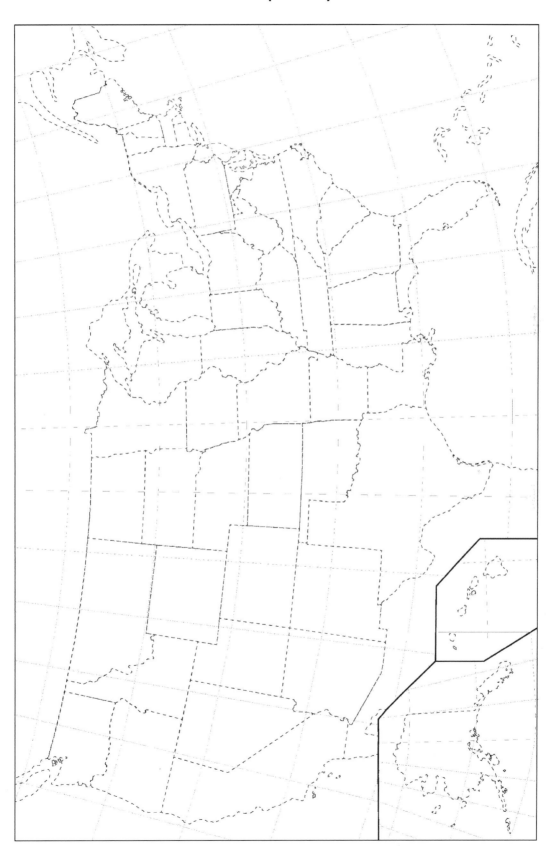

**Day 2:** On the map below, draw and label
all of the states and capitals you have learned.

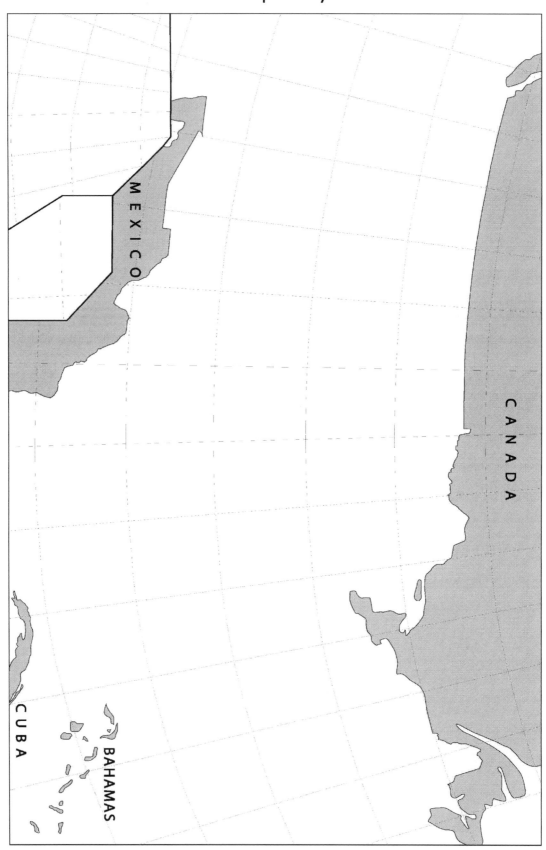

**Day 3:** On the map below, trace and label
all of the states and capitals you have learned.

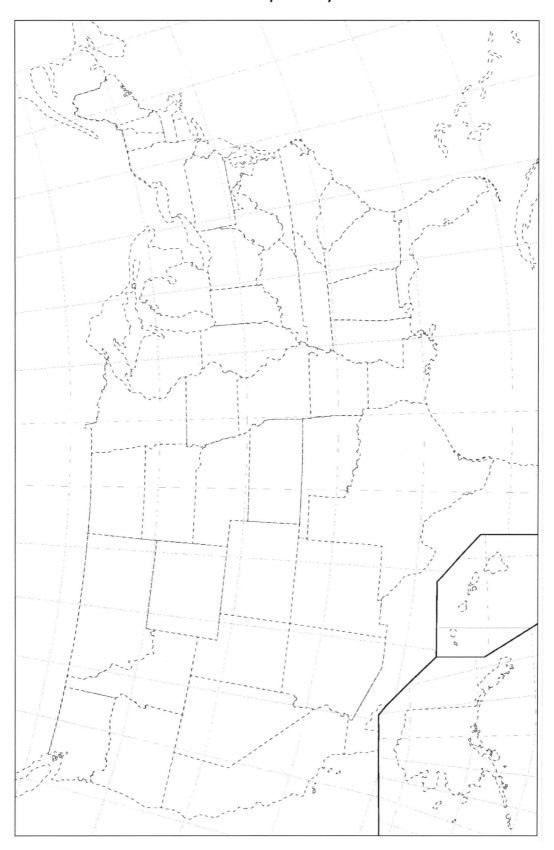

**Day 3:** On the map below, draw and label
all of the states and capitals you have learned.

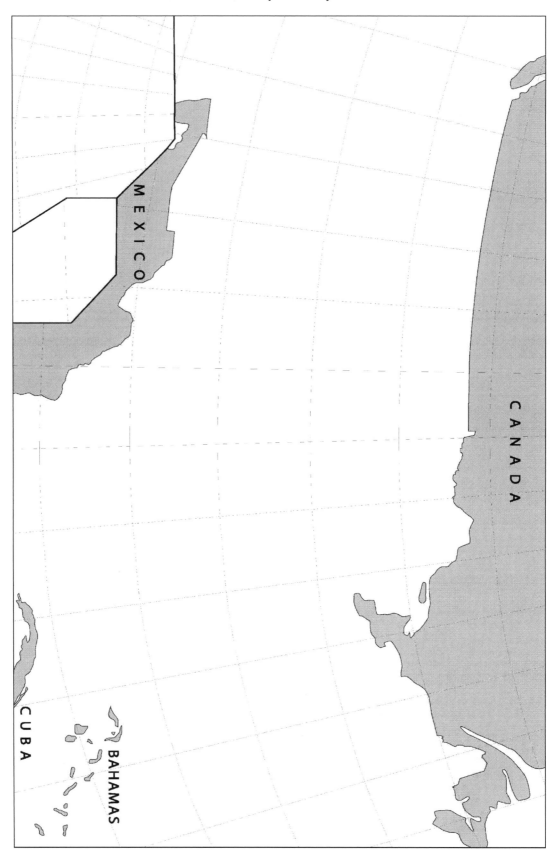

**Day 4:** On the lines below, list all of the states you have learned. On the small line, write the state abbreviation.

_____ _____
_____ _____
_____ _____
_____ _____
_____ _____
_____ _____
_____ _____
_____ _____
_____ _____
_____ _____

_____ _____
_____ _____
_____ _____
_____ _____
_____ _____
_____ _____

**Day 4:** On the map below, draw and label all of the states and capitals you have learned. Draw them without looking back.

# Alabama

Trace the state.
Draw it in the box below.

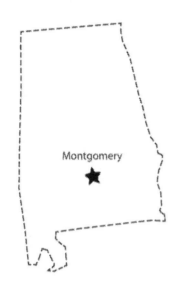

Montgomery

## State Facts

| | |
|---|---|
| Capital/Abbreviation | / |
| Area/Population | / |
| Statehood | |
| Bird/Flower | / |
| Industry | |
| Interesting Fact | |

# Mississippi

Trace the state.
Draw it in the box below.

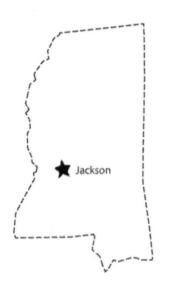

## State Facts

| | |
|---|---|
| Capital/Abbreviation | / |
| Area/Population | / |
| Statehood | |
| Bird/Flower | / |
| Industry | |
| Interesting Fact | |

**Day 1:** On the map below, trace and label
the new state and capital (or states and capitals) you have learned.

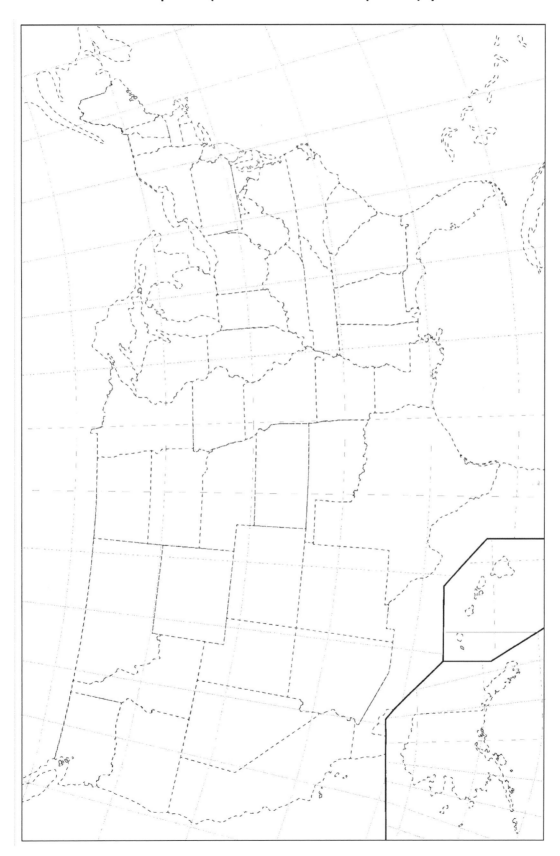

**Day 1:** On the map below, draw and label the new state (or states) you have learned. Add the capital(s).

**Day 2:** On the map below, trace and label all of the states and capitals you have learned.

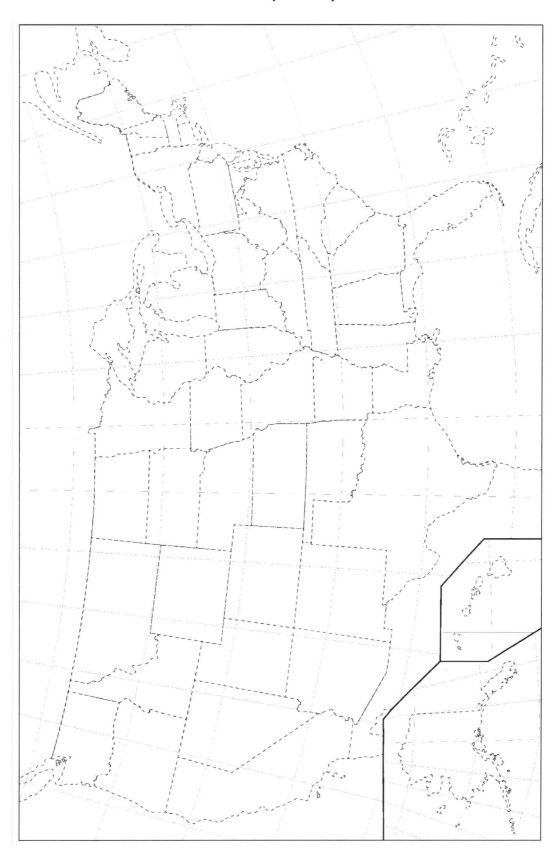

**Day 2:** On the map below, draw and label
all of the states and capitals you have learned.

**Day 3:** On the map below, trace and label
all of the states and capitals you have learned.

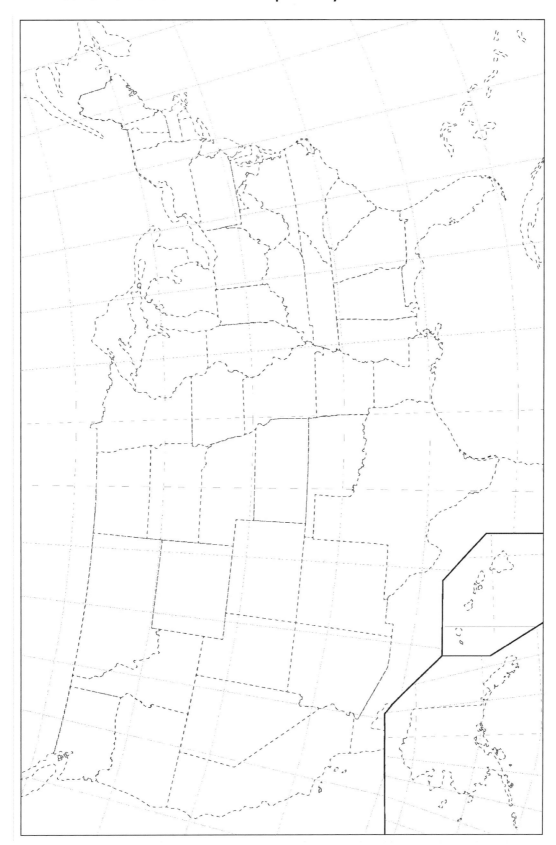

**Day 3:** On the map below, draw and label
all of the states and capitals you have learned.

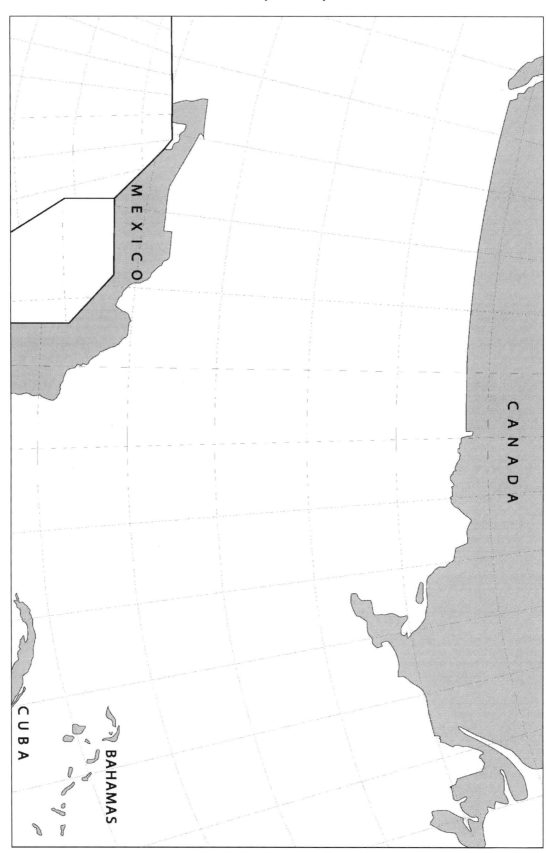

**Day 4:** On the lines below, list all of the states you have learned. On the small line, write the state abbreviation.

_____ _____    _____ _____

_____ _____    _____ _____

_____ _____    _____ _____

_____ _____    _____ _____

_____ _____    _____ _____

_____ _____    _____ _____

_____ _____    _____ _____

_____ _____    _____ _____

_____ _____    _____ _____

_____ _____

_____ _____

**Day 4:** On the map below, draw and label all of the states and capitals you have learned. Draw them without looking back.

# Tennessee

Trace the state.
Draw it in the box below.

## State Facts

| | |
|---|---|
| Capital/Abbreviation | / |
| Area/Population | / |
| Statehood | |
| Bird/Flower | / |
| Industry | |
| Interesting Fact | |

# Kentucky

## Trace the state.
## Draw it in the box below.

## State Facts

| | |
|---|---|
| Capital/Abbreviation | / |
| Area/Population | / |
| Statehood | |
| Bird/Flower | / |
| Industry | |
| Interesting Fact | |

**Day 1:** On the map below, trace and label
the new state and capital (or states and capitals) you have learned.

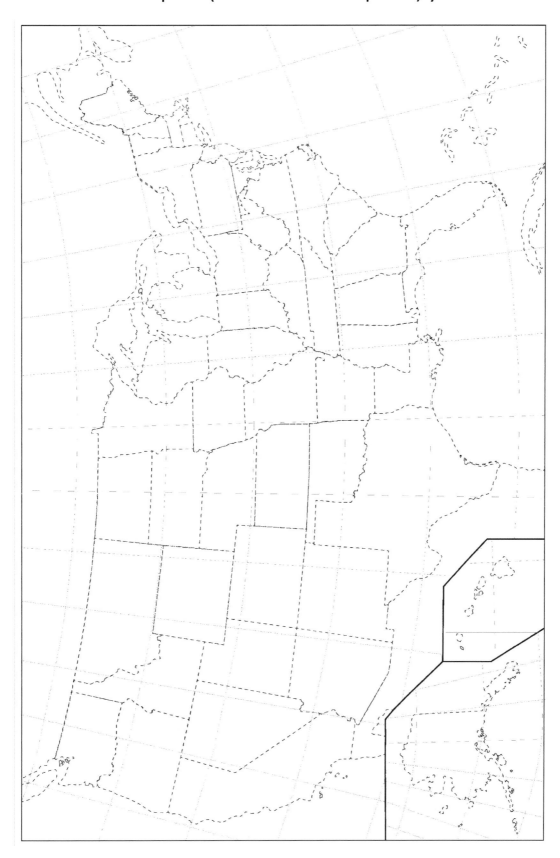

**Day 1:** On the map below, draw and label the new state (or states) you have learned. Add the capital(s).

**Day 2:** On the map below, trace and label
all of the states and capitals you have learned.

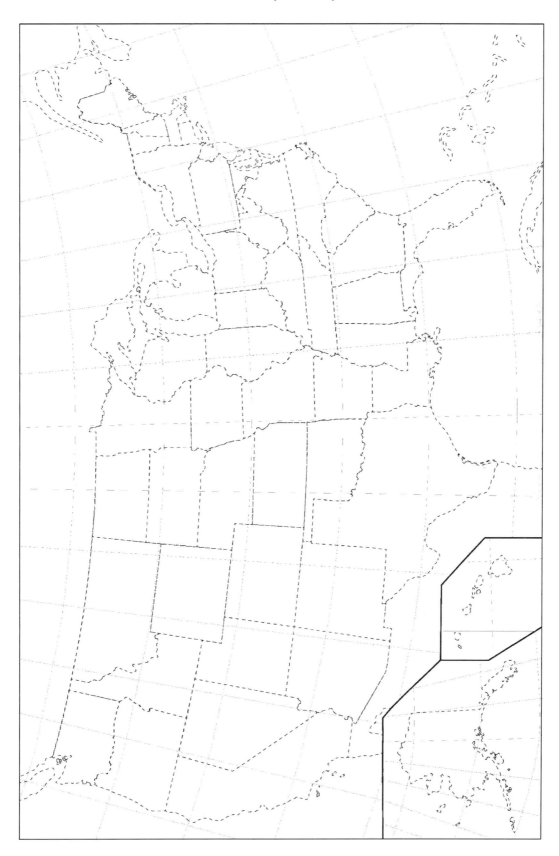

**Day 2:** On the map below, draw and label
all of the states and capitals you have learned.

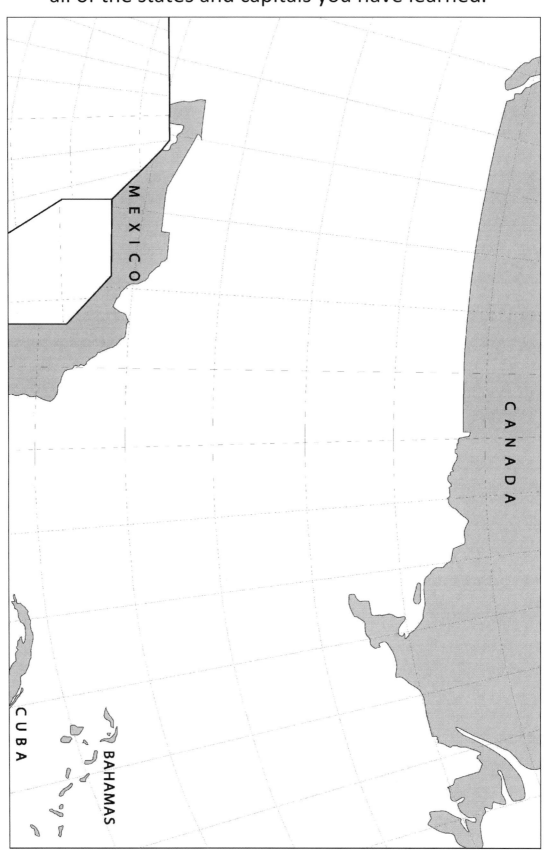

**Day 3:** On the map below, trace and label all of the states and capitals you have learned.

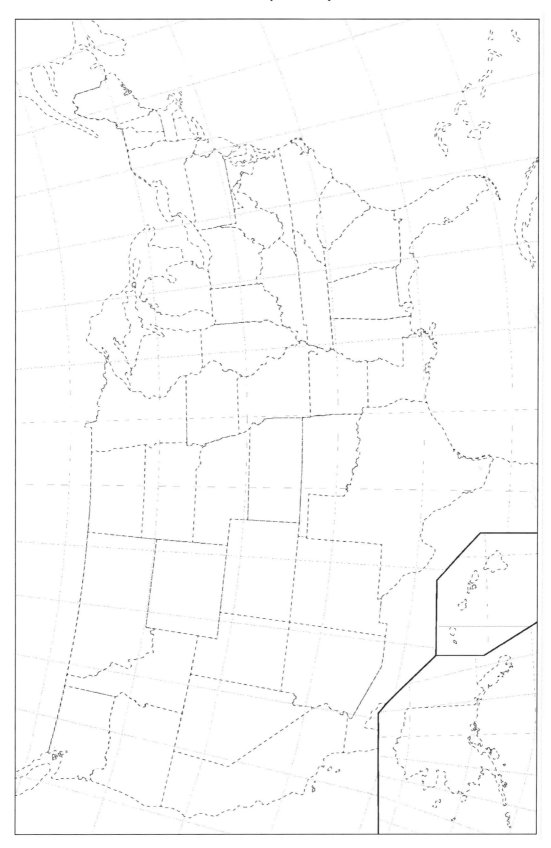

**Day 3:** On the map below, draw and label
all of the states and capitals you have learned.

**Day 4:** On the lines below, list all of the states you have learned. On the small line, write the state abbreviation.

**Day 4:** On the map below, draw and label all of the states and capitals you have learned. Draw them without looking back.

# Ohio

Trace the state.
Draw it in the box below.

Columbus

## State Facts

| | |
|---|---|
| Capital/Abbreviation | / |
| Area/Population | / |
| Statehood | |
| Bird/Flower | / |
| Industry | |
| Interesting Fact | |

**Day 1:** On the map below, trace and label
the new state and capital (or states and capitals) you have learned.

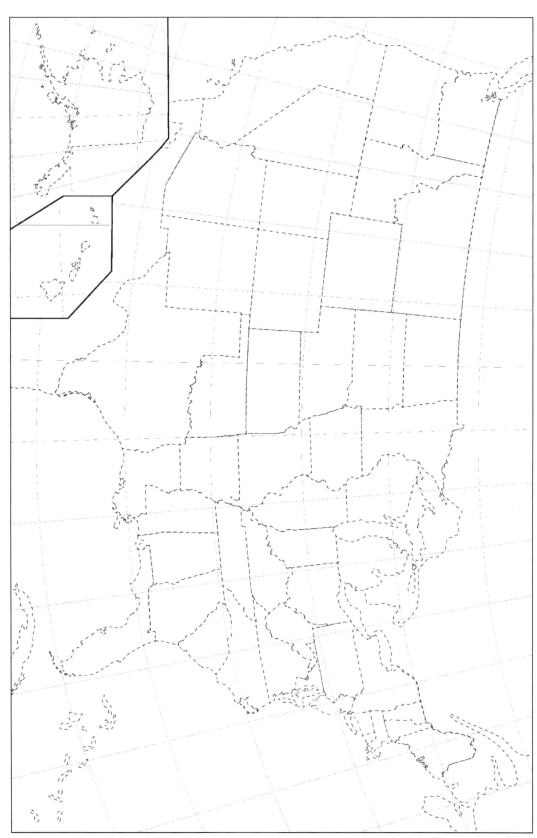

**Day 1:** On the map below, draw and label
the new state (or states) you have learned. Add the capital(s).

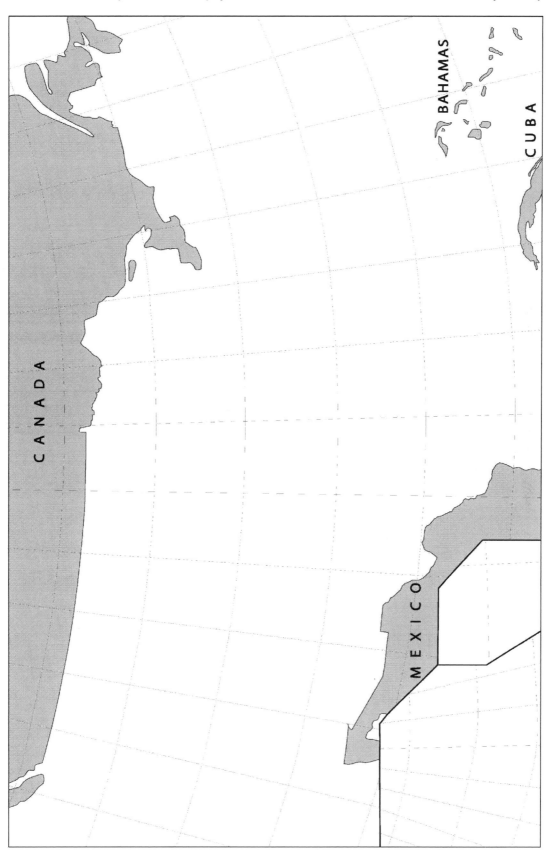

**Day 2:** On the map below, trace and label
all of the states and capitals you have learned.

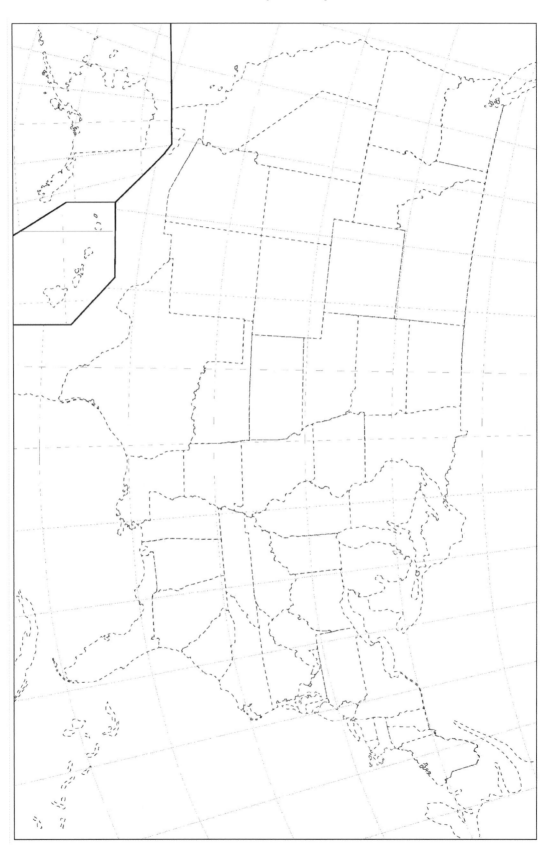

**Day 2:** On the map below, draw and label all of the states and capitals you have learned.

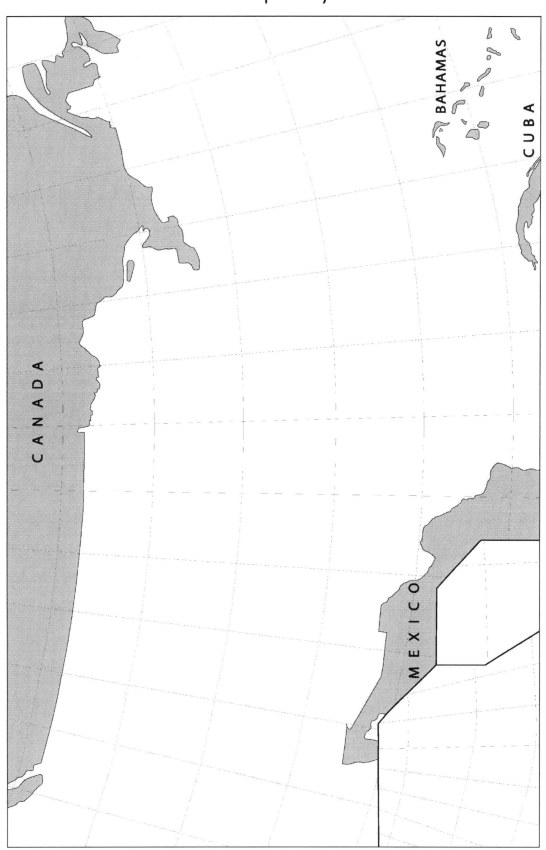

**Day 3:** On the map below, trace and label
all of the states and capitals you have learned.

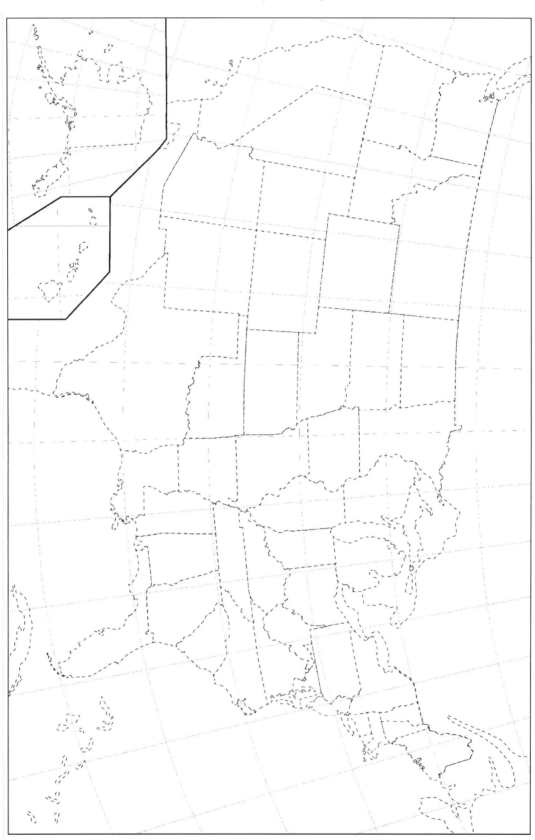

**Day 3:** On the map below, draw and label
all of the states and capitals you have learned.

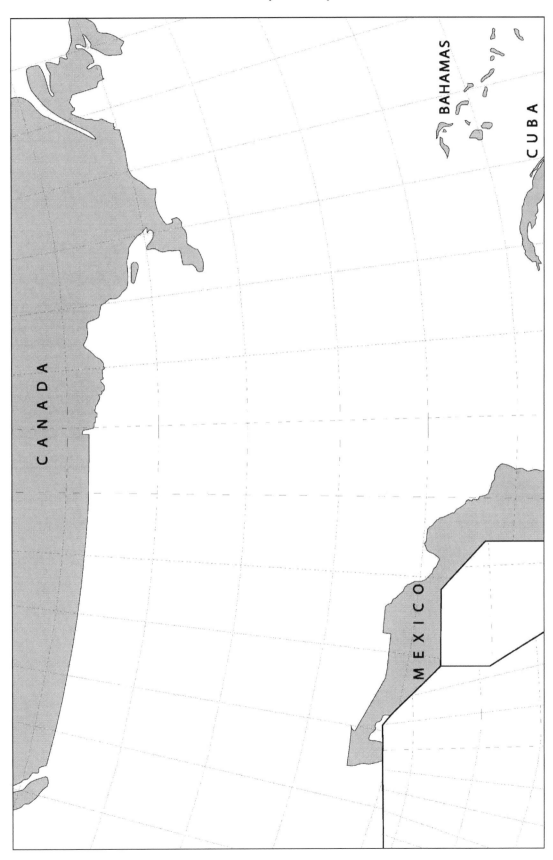

**Day 4:** On the lines below, list all of the states you have learned. On the small line, write the state abbreviation.

**Day 4:** On the map below, draw and label all of the states and capitals you have learned. Draw them without looking back.

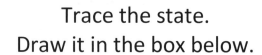

## Michigan

Trace the state.
Draw it in the box below.

Lansing

## State Facts

| | |
|---|---|
| Capital/Abbreviation | / |
| Area/Population | / |
| Statehood | |
| Bird/Flower | / |
| Industry | |
| Interesting Fact | |

**Day 1:** On the map below, trace and label
the new state and capital (or states and capitals) you have learned.

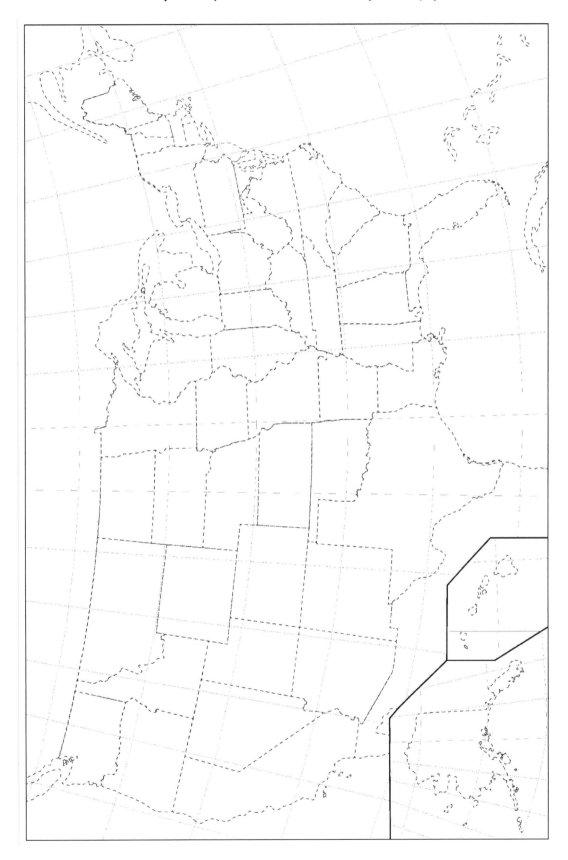

**Day 1:** On the map below, draw and label
the new state (or states) you have learned. Add the capital(s).

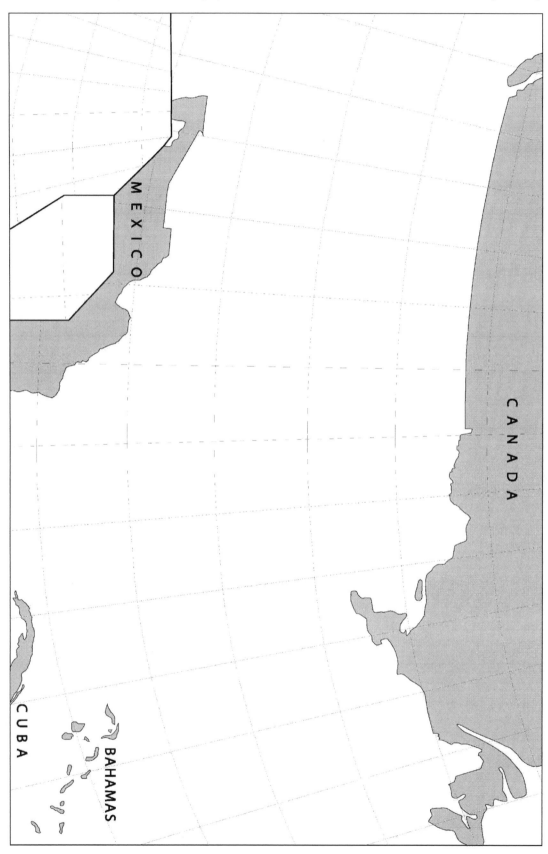

**Day 2:** On the map below, trace and label all of the states and capitals you have learned.

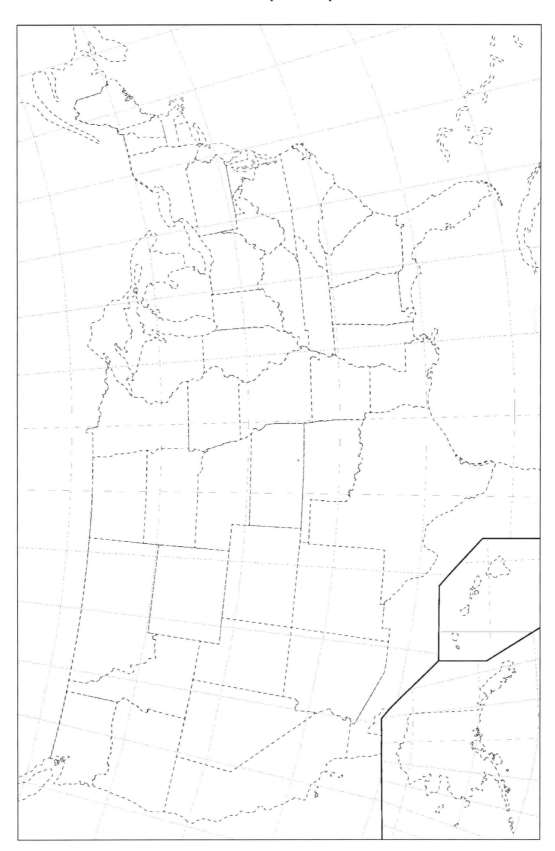

**Day 2:** On the map below, draw and label
all of the states and capitals you have learned.

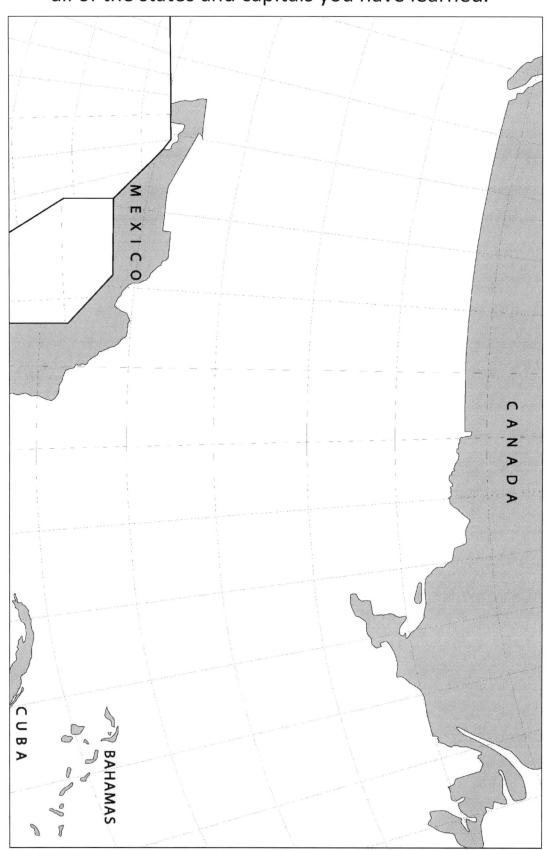

**Day 3:** On the map below, trace and label
all of the states and capitals you have learned.

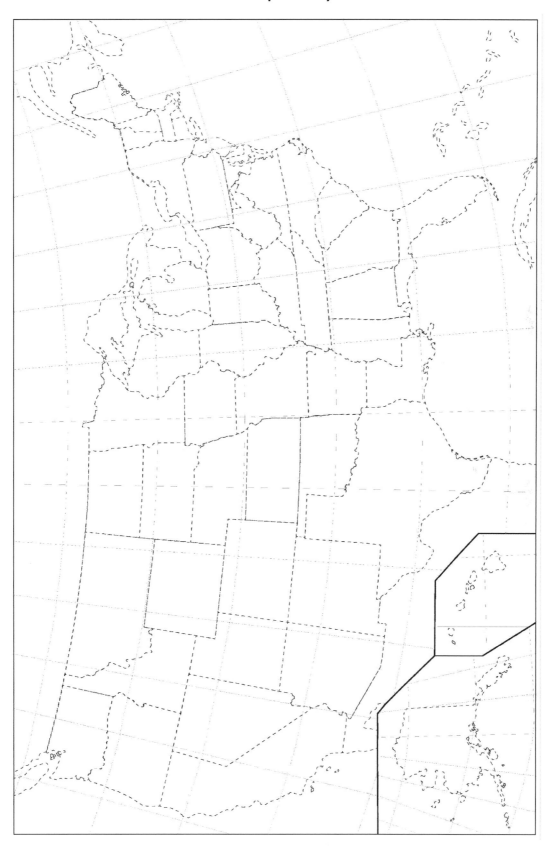

**Day 3:** On the map below, draw and label
all of the states and capitals you have learned.

**Day 4:** On the lines below, list all of the states you have learned. On the small line, write the state abbreviation.

_____   _____          _____   _____

_____   _____          _____   _____

_____   _____          _____   _____

_____   _____          _____   _____

_____   _____          _____   _____

_____   _____          _____   _____

_____   _____          _____   _____

_____   _____          _____   _____

_____   _____          _____   _____

_____   _____          _____   _____

_____   _____          _____   _____

_____   _____

_____   _____

**Day 4:** On the map below, draw and label all of the states and capitals you have learned. Draw them without looking back.

# Indiana

Indianapolis

Trace the state.
Draw it in the box below.

## State Facts

| | |
|---|---|
| Capital/Abbreviation | / |
| Area/Population | / |
| Statehood | |
| Bird/Flower | / |
| Industry | |
| Interesting Fact | |

**Day 1:** On the map below, trace and label
the new state and capital (or states and capitals) you have learned.

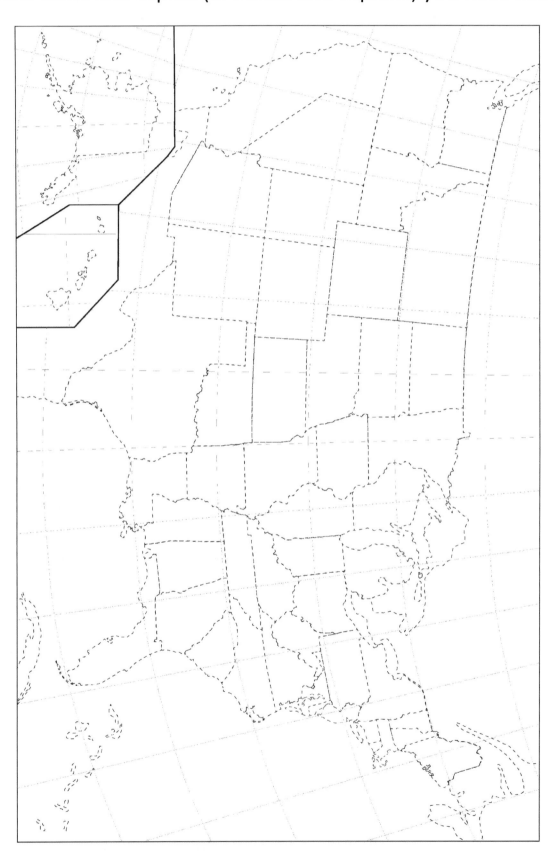

**Day 1:** On the map below, draw and label
the new state (or states) you have learned. Add the capital(s).

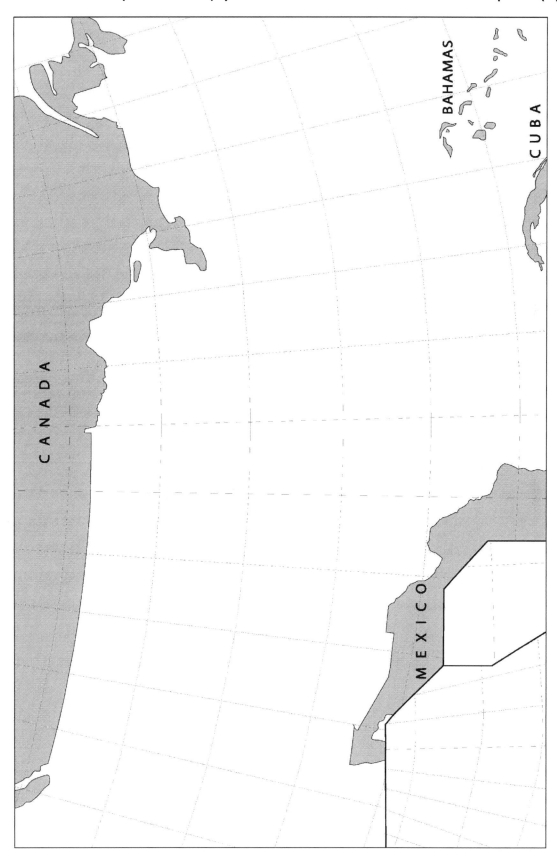

**Day 2:** On the map below, trace and label
all of the states and capitals you have learned.

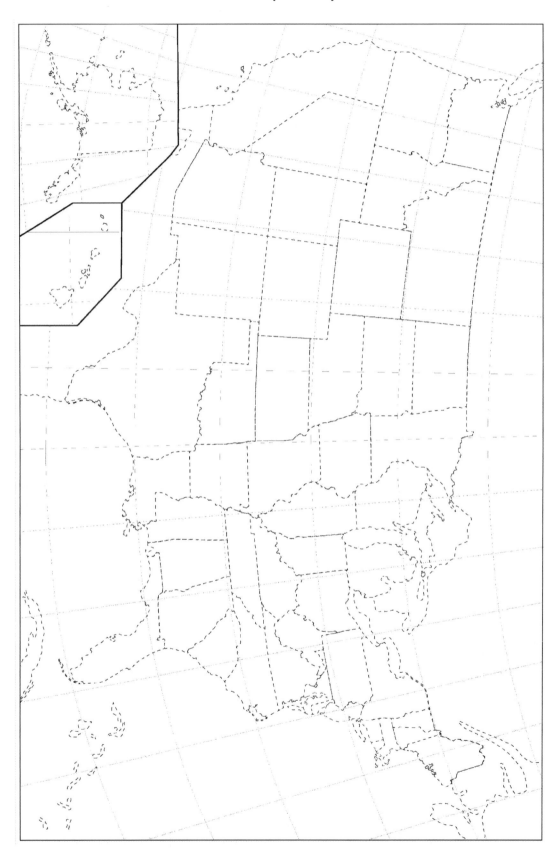

**Day 2:** On the map below, draw and label
all of the states and capitals you have learned.

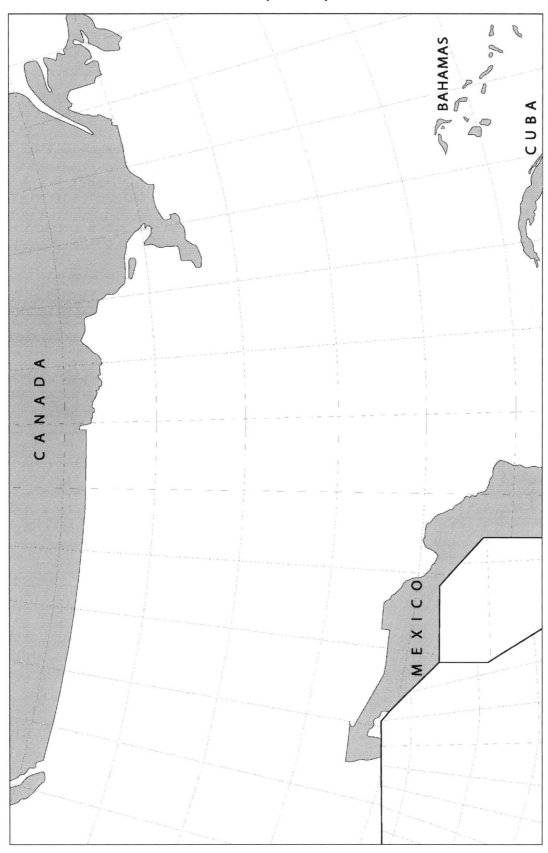

**Day 3:** On the map below, trace and label
all of the states and capitals you have learned.

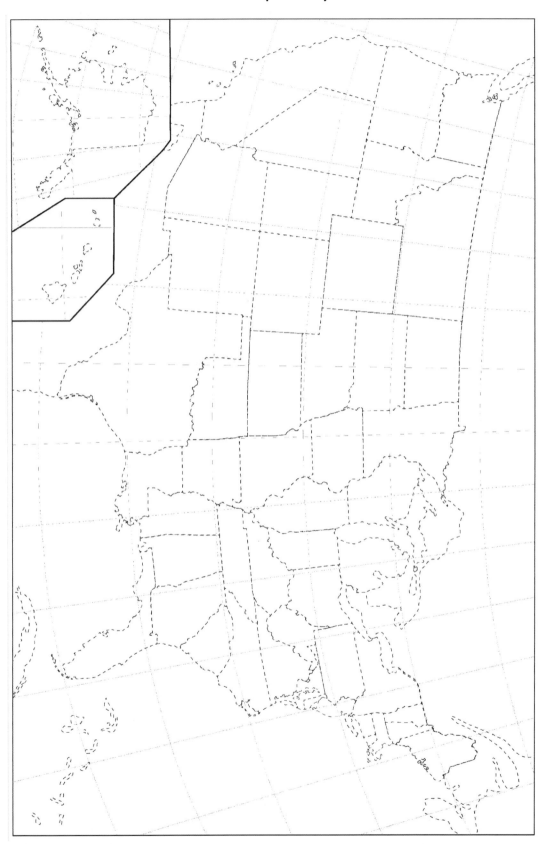

**Day 3:** On the map below, draw and label
all of the states and capitals you have learned.

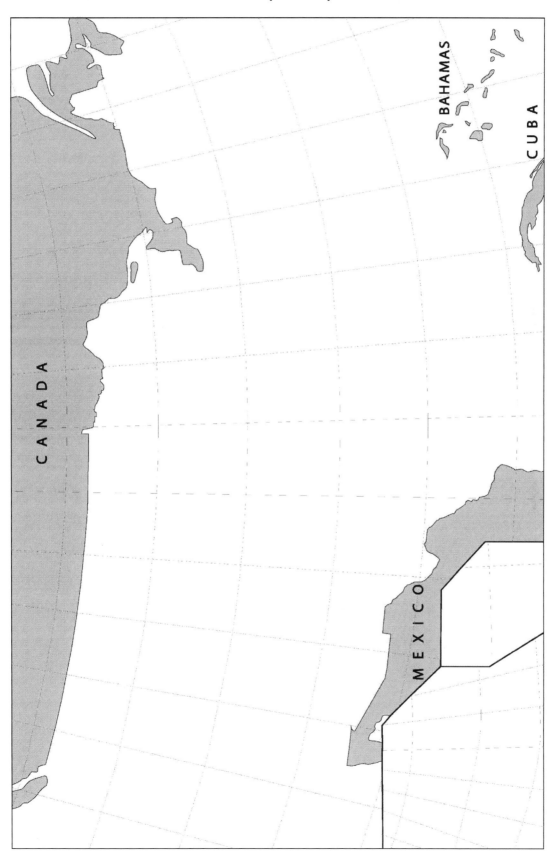

**Day 4:** On the lines below, list all of the states you have learned. On the small line, write the state abbreviation.

**Day 4:** On the map below, draw and label all of the states and capitals you have learned. Draw them without looking back.

# Illinois

Trace the state.
Draw it in the box below.

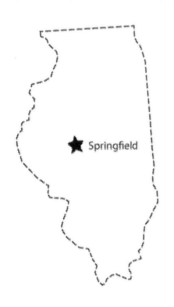

## State Facts

| | |
|---|---|
| Capital/Abbreviation | / |
| Area/Population | / |
| Statehood | |
| Bird/Flower | / |
| Industry | |
| Interesting Fact | |

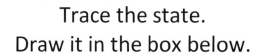

Trace the state.
Draw it in the box below.

## State Facts

| | |
|---|---|
| Capital/Abbreviation | / |
| Area/Population | / |
| Statehood | |
| Bird/Flower | / |
| Industry | |
| Interesting Fact | |

**Day 1:** On the map below, trace and label
the new state and capital (or states and capitals) you have learned.

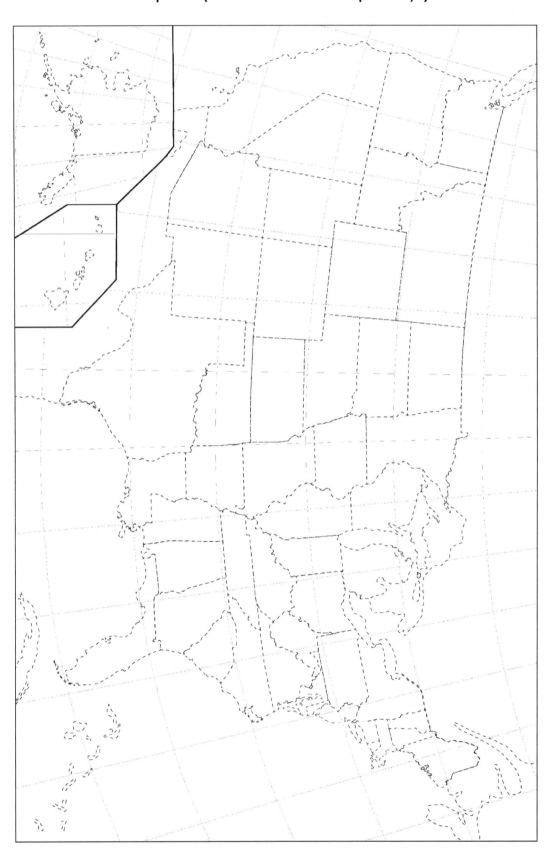

**Day 1:** On the map below, draw and label
the new state (or states) you have learned. Add the capital(s).

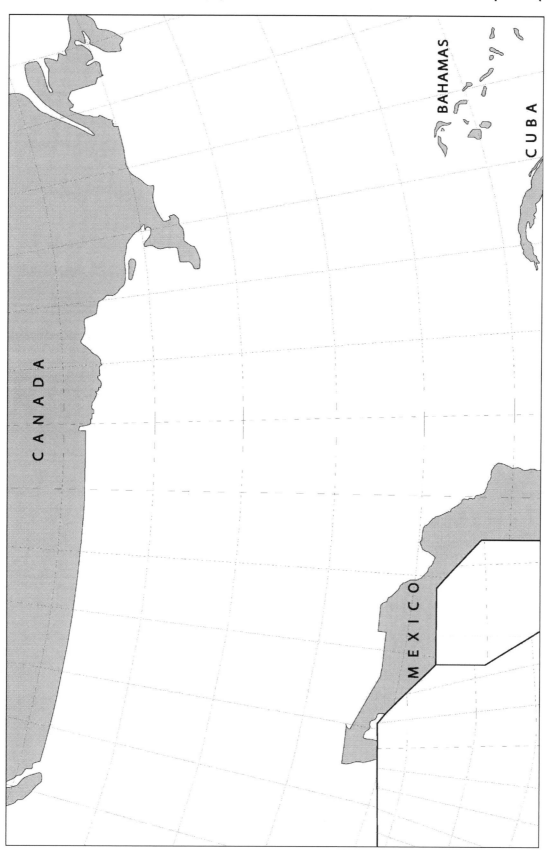

**Day 2:** On the map below, trace and label
all of the states and capitals you have learned.

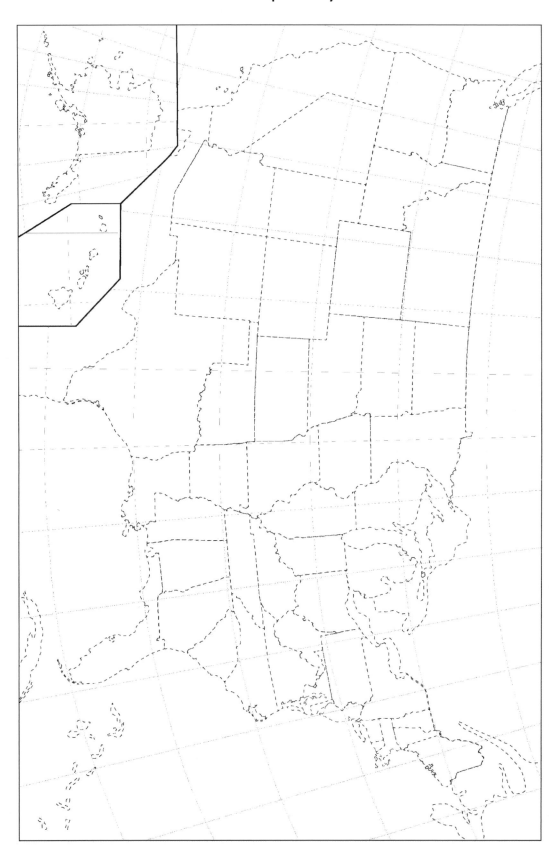

**Day 2:** On the map below, draw and label
all of the states and capitals you have learned.

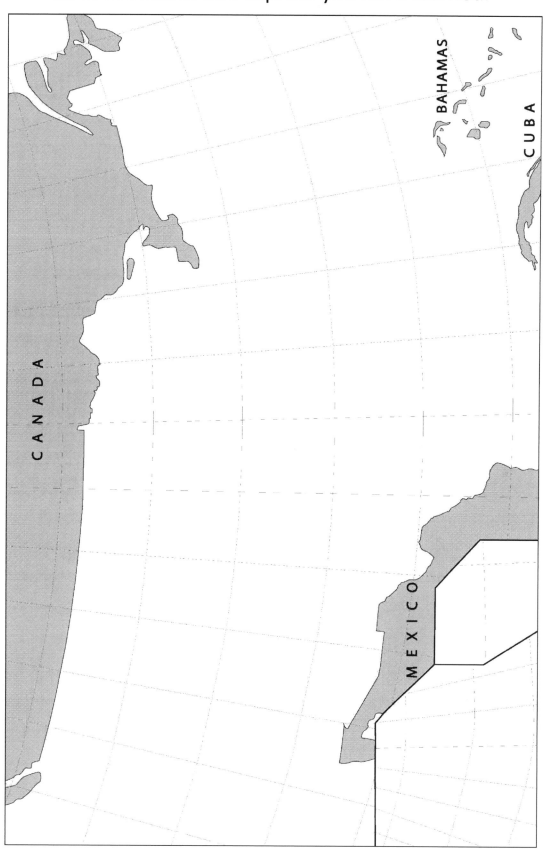

**Day 3:** On the map below, trace and label
all of the states and capitals you have learned.

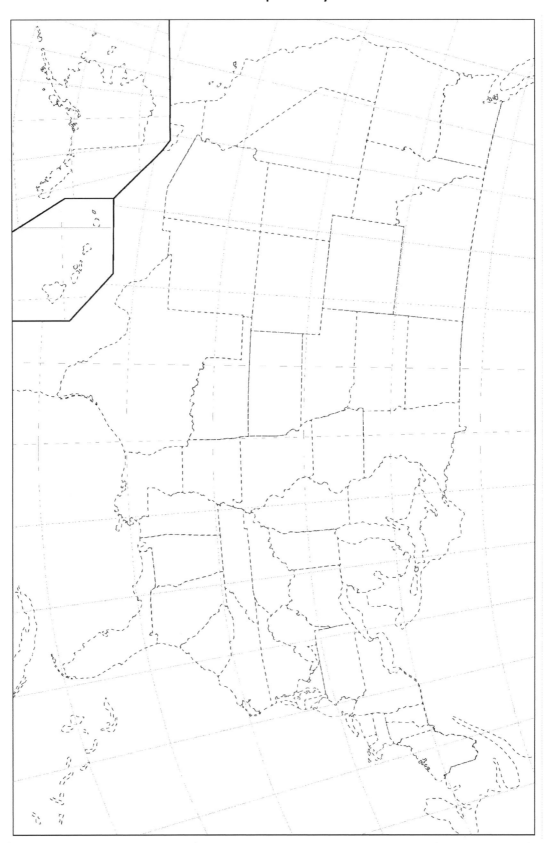

**Day 3:** On the map below, draw and label
all of the states and capitals you have learned.

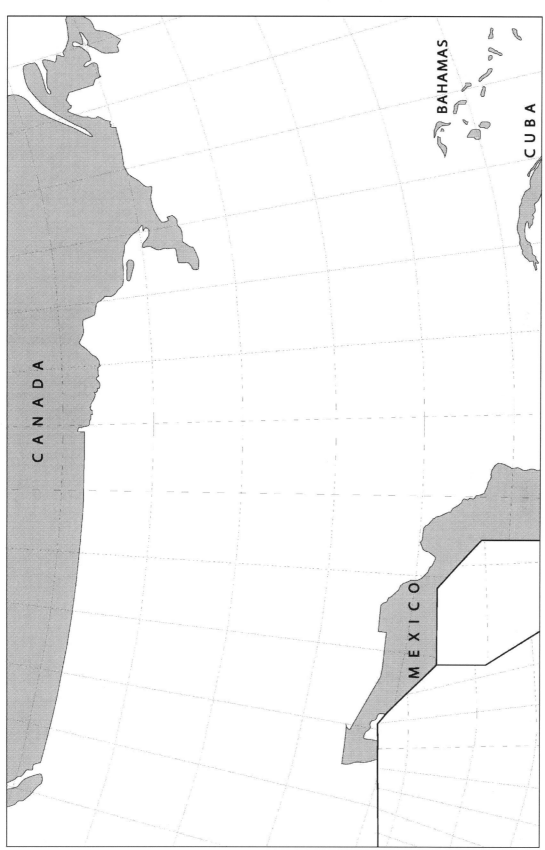

**Day 4:** On the lines below, list all of the states you have learned. On the small line, write the state abbreviation.

**Day 4:** On the map below, draw and label all of the states and capitals you have learned. Draw them without looking back.

# Minnesota

Trace the state.
Draw it in the box below.

St. Paul

## State Facts

| | |
|---|---|
| Capital/Abbreviation | / |
| Area/Population | / |
| Statehood | |
| Bird/Flower | / |
| Industry | |
| Interesting Fact | |

**Day 1:** On the map below, trace and label
the new state and capital (or states and capitals) you have learned.

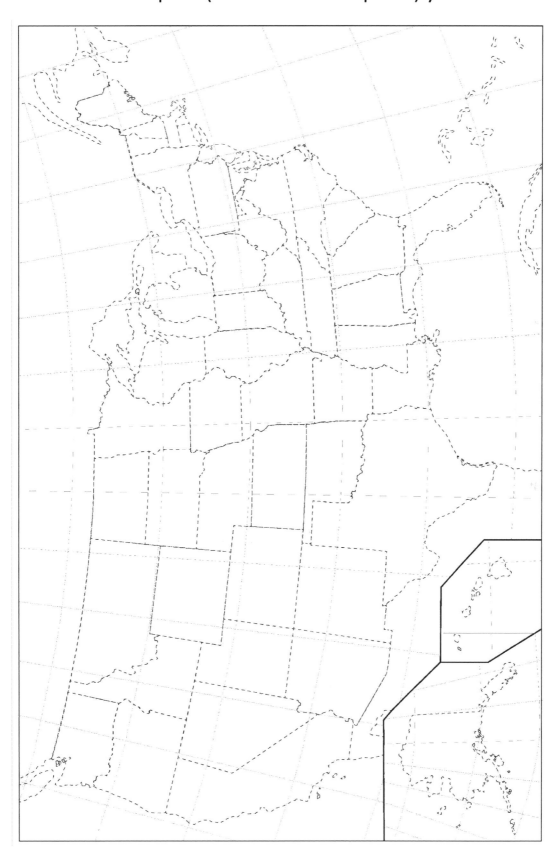

**Day 1:** On the map below, draw and label
the new state (or states) you have learned. Add the capital(s).

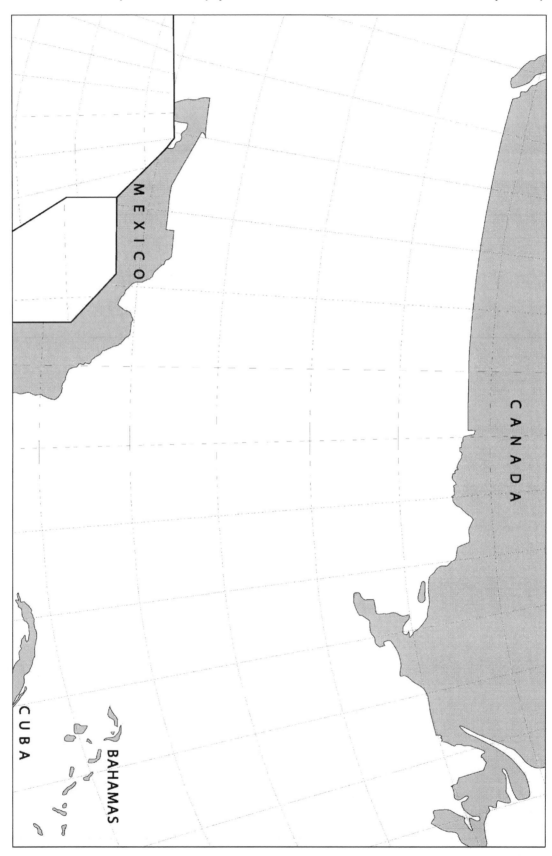

**Day 2:** On the map below, trace and label
all of the states and capitals you have learned.

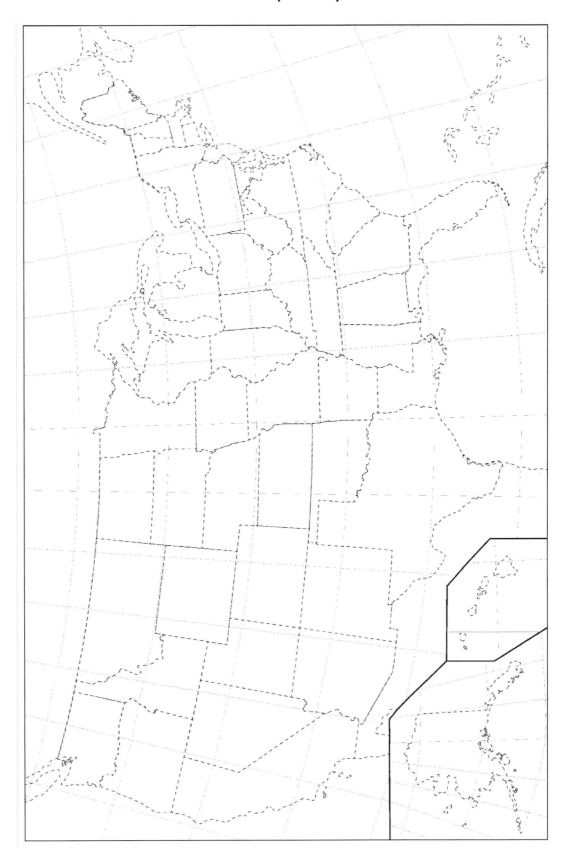

**Day 2:** On the map below, draw and label
all of the states and capitals you have learned.

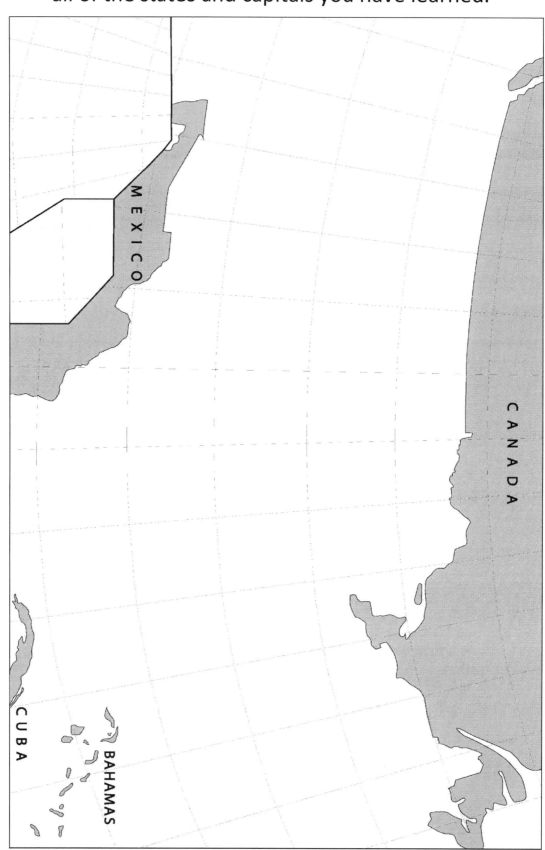

**Day 3:** On the map below, trace and label all of the states and capitals you have learned.

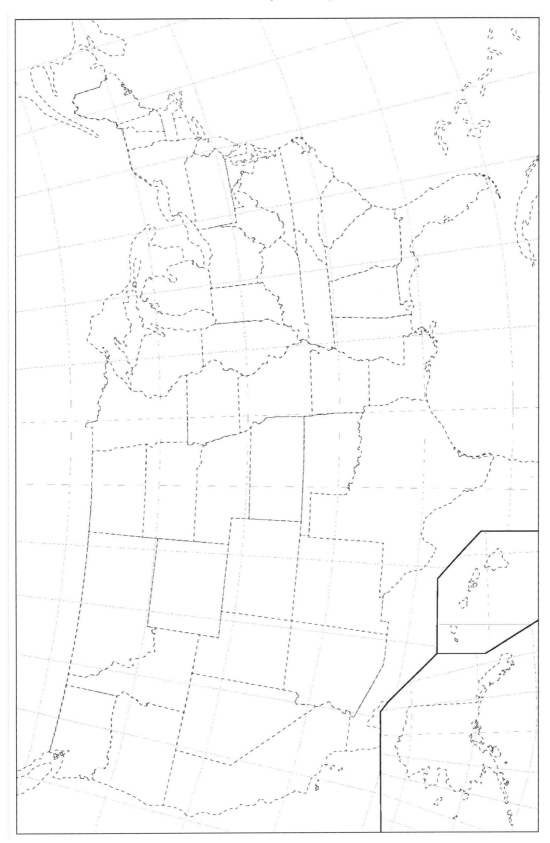

**Day 3:** On the map below, draw and label
all of the states and capitals you have learned.

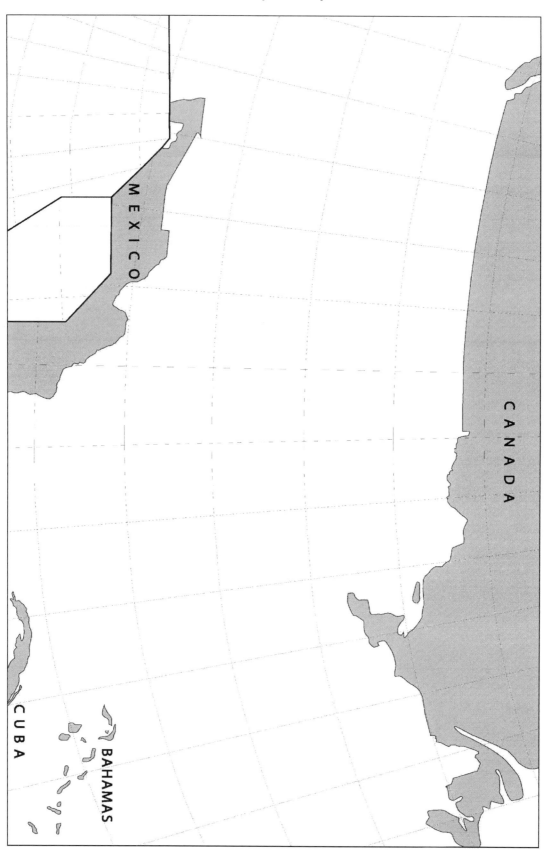

**Day 4:** On the lines below, list all of the states you have learned. On the small line, write the state abbreviation.

**Day 4:** On the map below, draw and label all of the states and capitals you have learned. Draw them without looking back.

# Iowa

Trace the state.
Draw it in the box below.

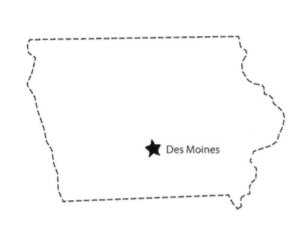

Des Moines

## State Facts

| | |
|---|---|
| Capital/Abbreviation | / |
| Area/Population | / |
| Statehood | |
| Bird/Flower | / |
| Industry | |
| Interesting Fact | |

# Missouri

Trace the state.
Draw it in the box below.

## State Facts

| | |
|---|---|
| Capital/Abbreviation | / |
| Area/Population | / |
| Statehood | |
| Bird/Flower | / |
| Industry | |
| Interesting Fact | |

# Arkansas

Trace the state.
Draw it in the box below.

## State Facts

| | |
|---|---|
| Capital/Abbreviation | / |
| Area/Population | / |
| Statehood | |
| Bird/Flower | / |
| Industry | |
| Interesting Fact | |

# Louisiana

Trace the state.
Draw it in the box below.

Baton Rouge

## State Facts

| Capital/Abbreviation | / |
|---|---|
| Area/Population | / |
| Statehood | |
| Bird/Flower | / |
| Industry | |
| Interesting Fact | |

**Day 1:** On the map below, trace and label
the new state and capital (or states and capitals) you have learned.

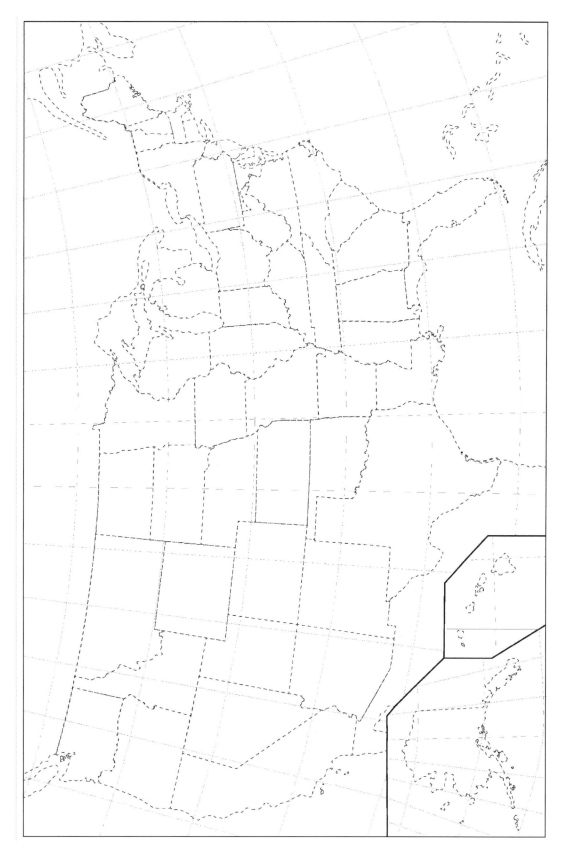

**Day 1:** On the map below, draw and label
the new state (or states) you have learned. Add the capital(s).

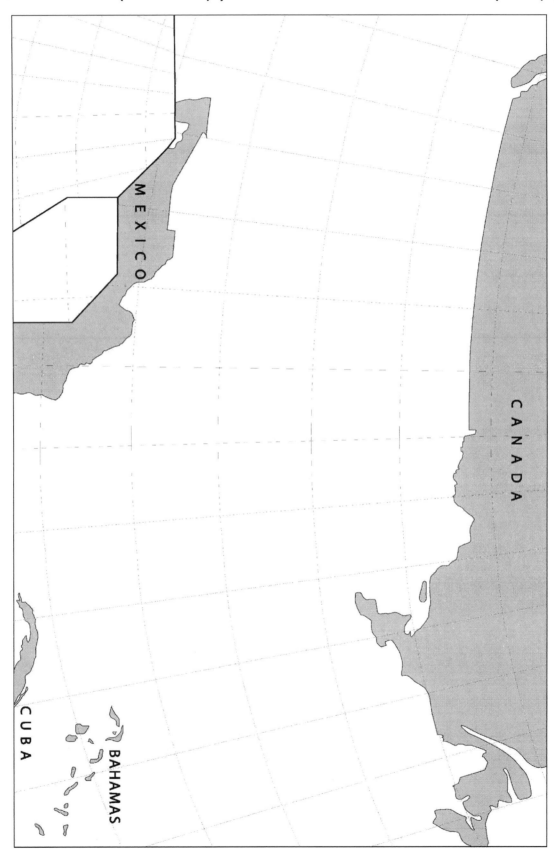

**Day 2:** On the map below, trace and label
all of the states and capitals you have learned.

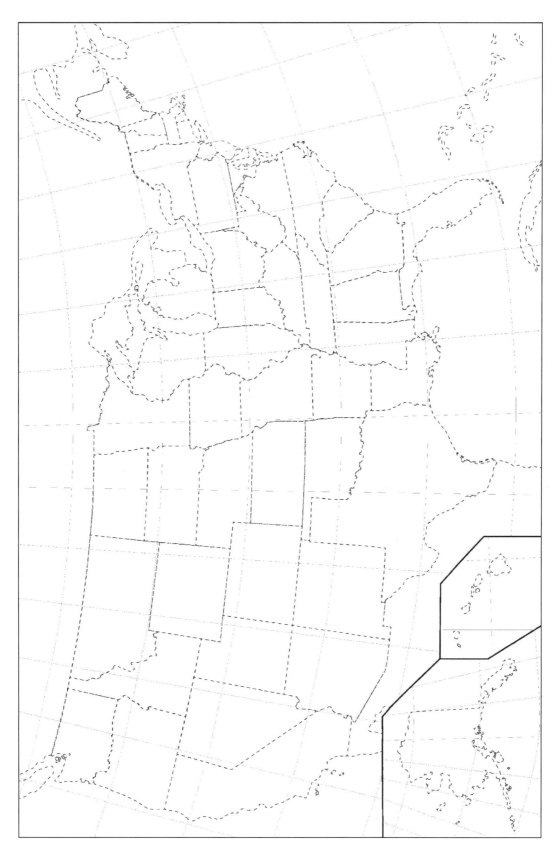

**Day 2:** On the map below, draw and label
all of the states and capitals you have learned.

**Day 3:** On the map below, trace and label
all of the states and capitals you have learned.

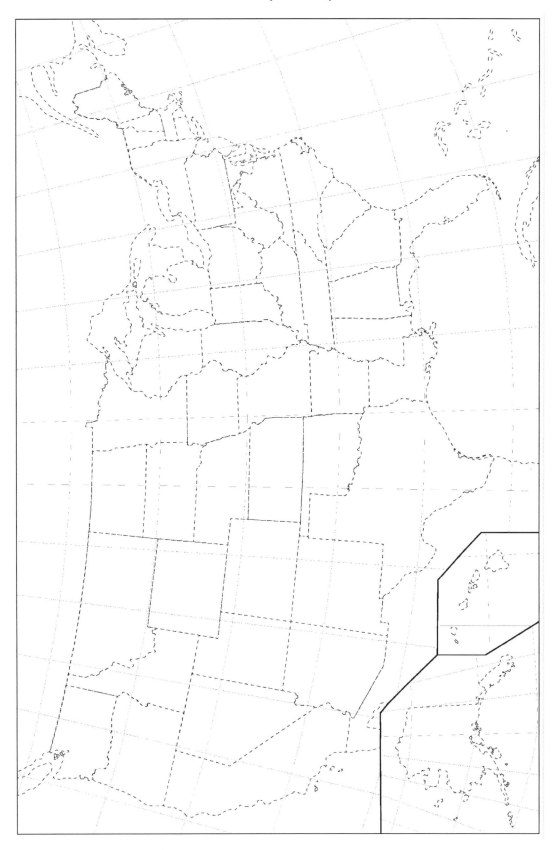

**Day 3:** On the map below, draw and label
all of the states and capitals you have learned.

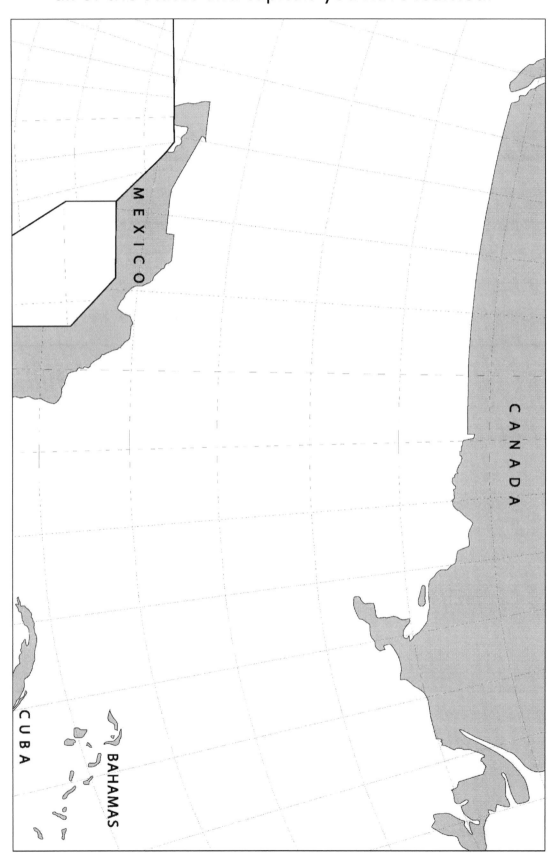

**Day 4:** On the lines below, list all of the states you have learned. On the small line, write the state abbreviation.

_____ _____
_____ _____
_____ _____
_____ _____
_____ _____
_____ _____
_____ _____
_____ _____
_____ _____
_____ _____
_____ _____
_____ _____
_____ _____
_____ _____
_____ _____
_____ _____

_____ _____
_____ _____
_____ _____
_____ _____
_____ _____
_____ _____
_____ _____
_____ _____
_____ _____
_____ _____
_____ _____
_____ _____

**Day 4:** On the map below, draw and label all of the states and capitals you have learned. Draw them without looking back.

# Texas

Trace the state.
Draw it in the box below.

## State Facts

| | |
|---|---|
| Capital/Abbreviation | / |
| Area/Population | / |
| Statehood | |
| Bird/Flower | / |
| Industry | |
| Interesting Fact | |

185

**Day 1:** On the map below, trace and label
the new state and capital (or states and capitals) you have learned.

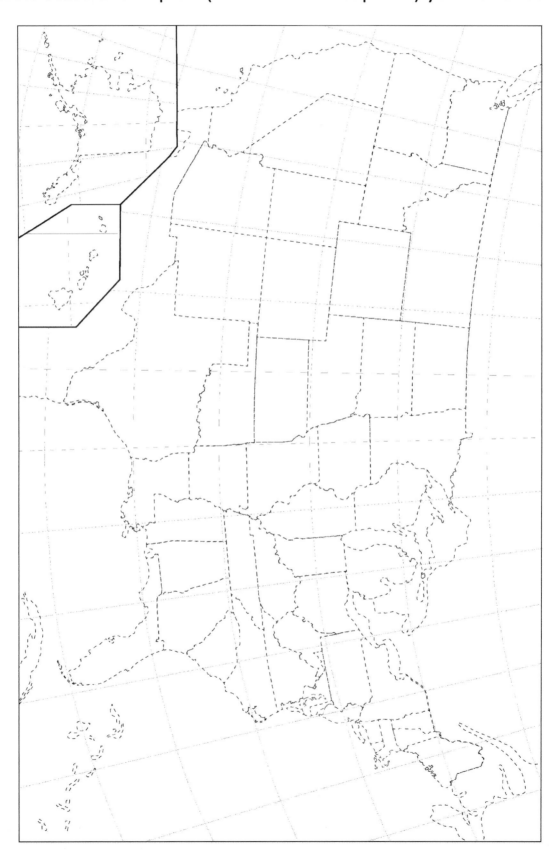

**Day 1:** On the map below, draw and label the new state (or states) you have learned. Add the capital(s).

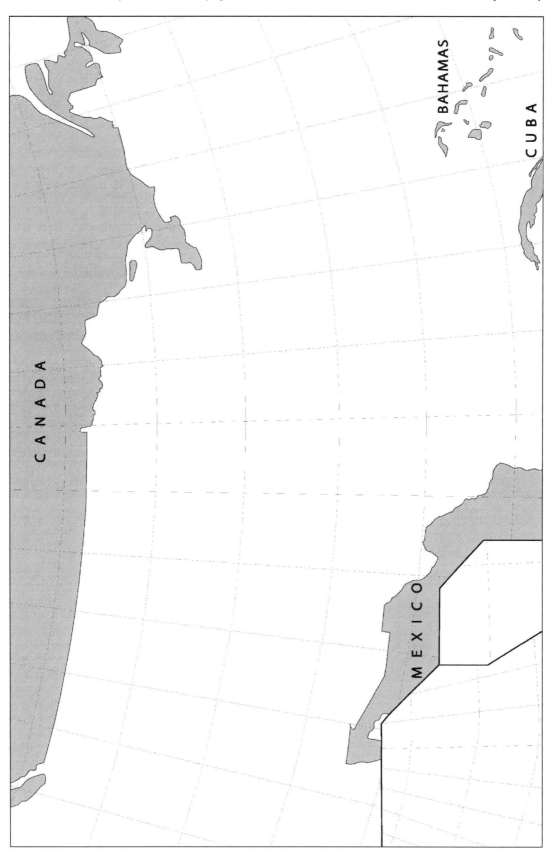

**Day 2:** On the map below, trace and label
all of the states and capitals you have learned.

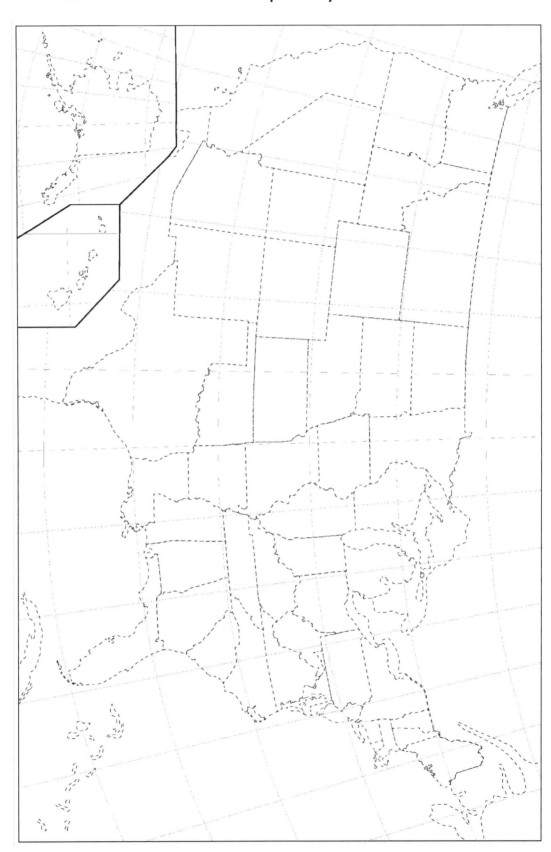

**Day 2:** On the map below, draw and label
all of the states and capitals you have learned.

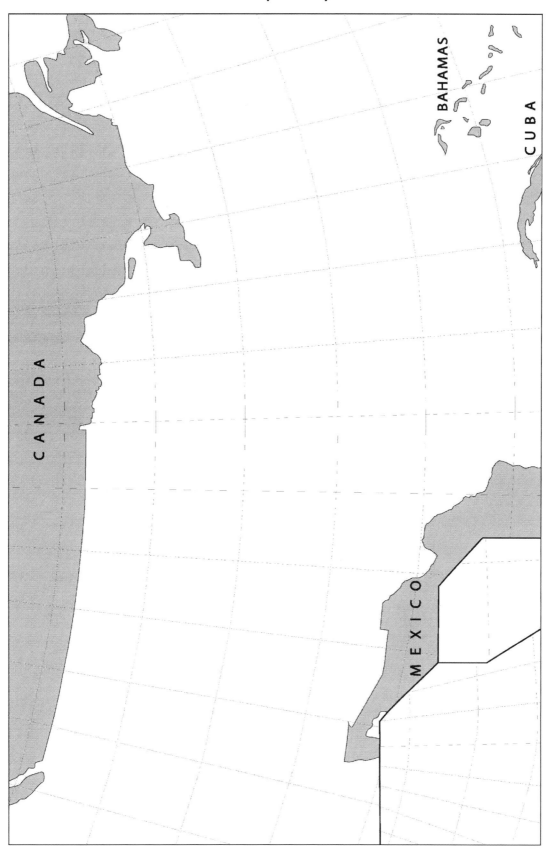

**Day 3:** On the map below, trace and label
all of the states and capitals you have learned.

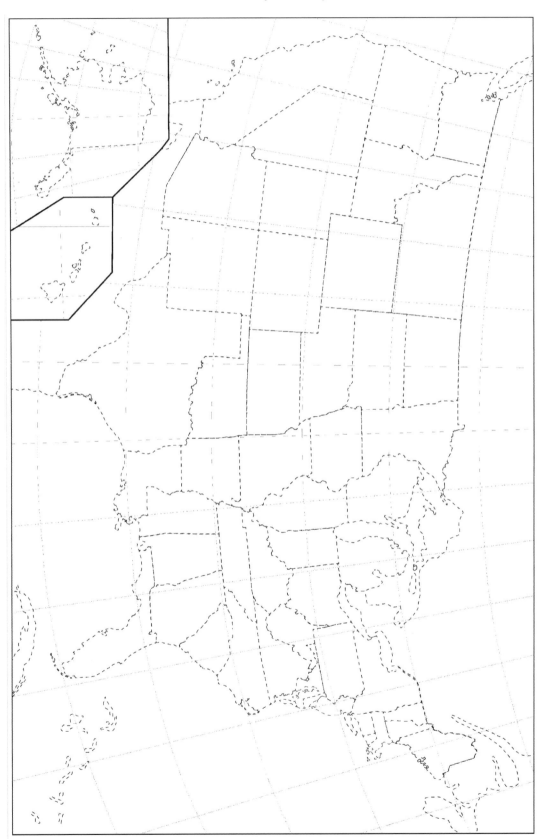

**Day 3:** On the map below, draw and label
all of the states and capitals you have learned.

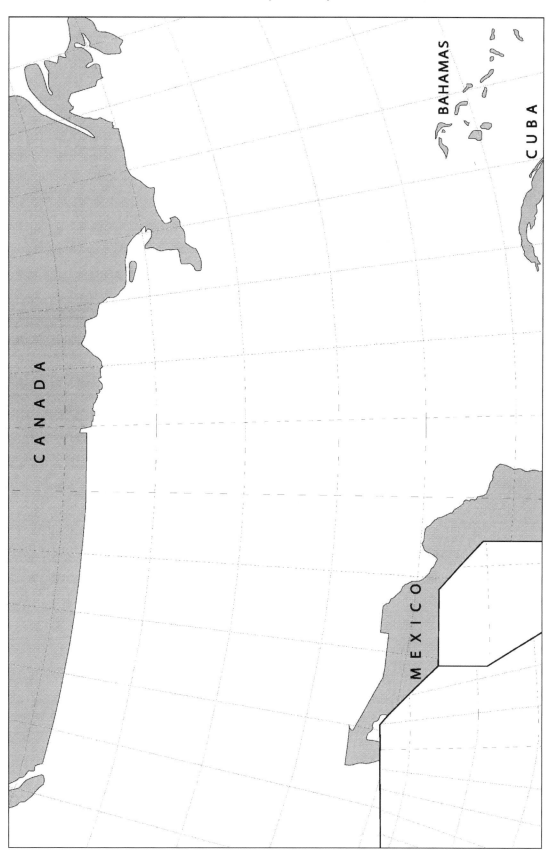

**Day 4:** On the lines below, list all of the states you have learned. On the small line, write the state abbreviation.

_____ _____

_____ _____

_____ _____

_____ _____

_____ _____

_____ _____

_____ _____

_____ _____

_____ _____

_____ _____

_____ _____

_____ _____

_____ _____

_____ _____

_____ _____

_____ _____

**Day 4:** On the map below, draw and label all of the states and capitals you have learned. Draw them without looking back.

# Oklahoma

Trace the state.
Draw it in the box below.

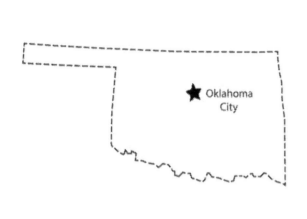

Oklahoma City

## State Facts

| | |
|---|---|
| Capital/Abbreviation | / |
| Area/Population | / |
| Statehood | |
| Bird/Flower | / |
| Industry | |
| Interesting Fact | |

# Kansas

Trace the state.
Draw it in the box below.

## State Facts

| | |
|---|---|
| Capital/Abbreviation | / |
| Area/Population | / |
| Statehood | |
| Bird/Flower | / |
| Industry | |
| Interesting Fact | |

# Nebraska

Trace the state.
Draw it in the box below.

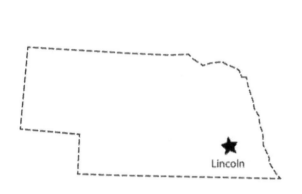

## State Facts

| | |
|---|---|
| Capital/Abbreviation | / |
| Area/Population | / |
| Statehood | |
| Bird/Flower | / |
| Industry | |
| Interesting Fact | |

**Day 1:** On the map below, trace and label
the new state and capital (or states and capitals) you have learned.

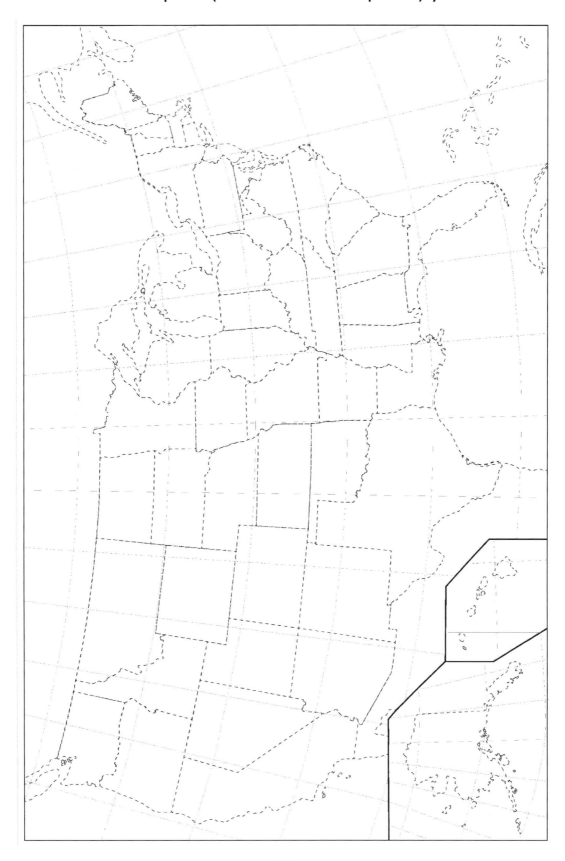

**Day 1:** On the map below, draw and label
the new state (or states) you have learned. Add the capital(s).

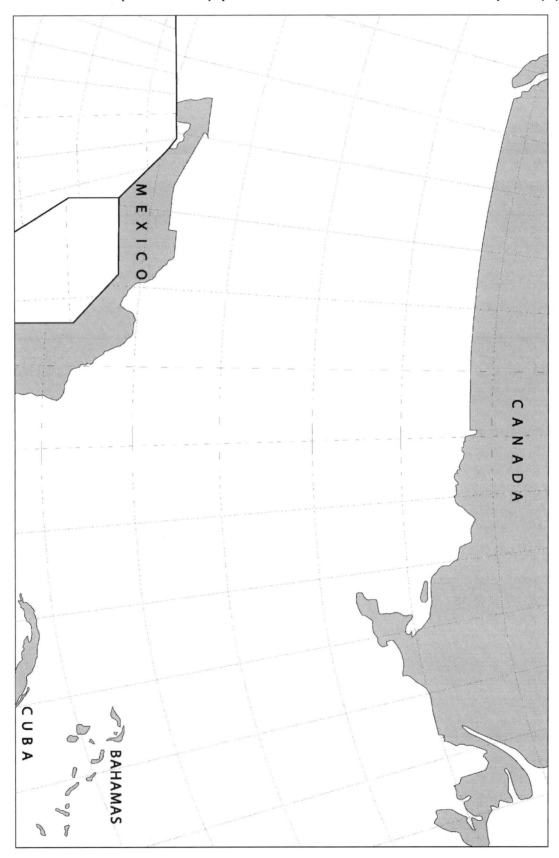

**Day 2:** On the map below, trace and label
all of the states and capitals you have learned.

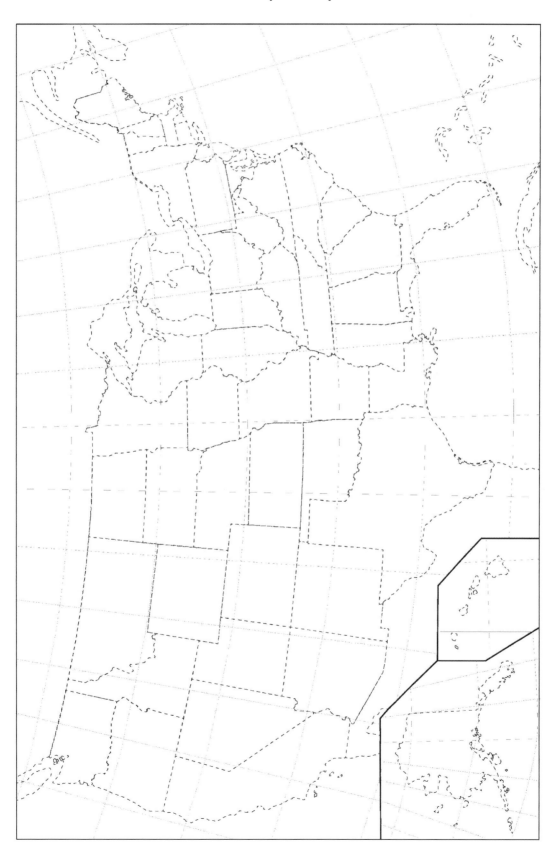

**Day 2:** On the map below, draw and label
all of the states and capitals you have learned.

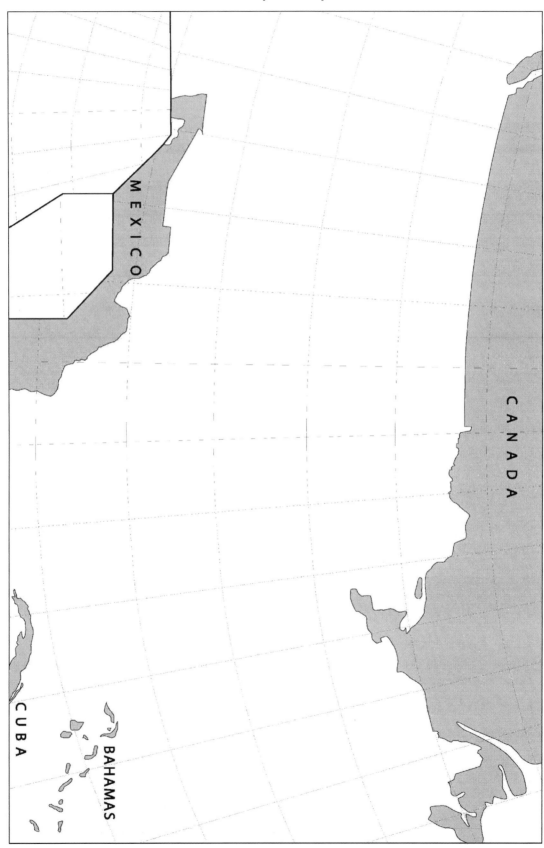

**Day 3:** On the map below, trace and label
all of the states and capitals you have learned.

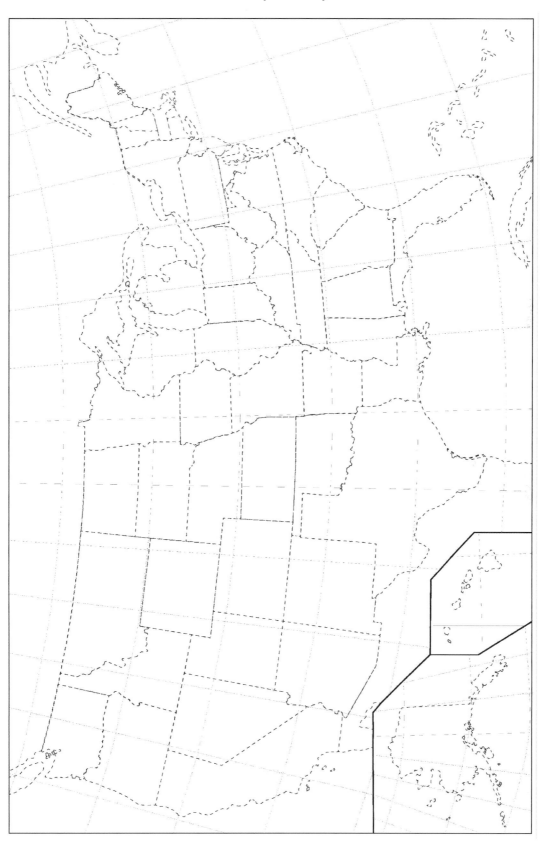

**Day 3:** On the map below, draw and label
all of the states and capitals you have learned.

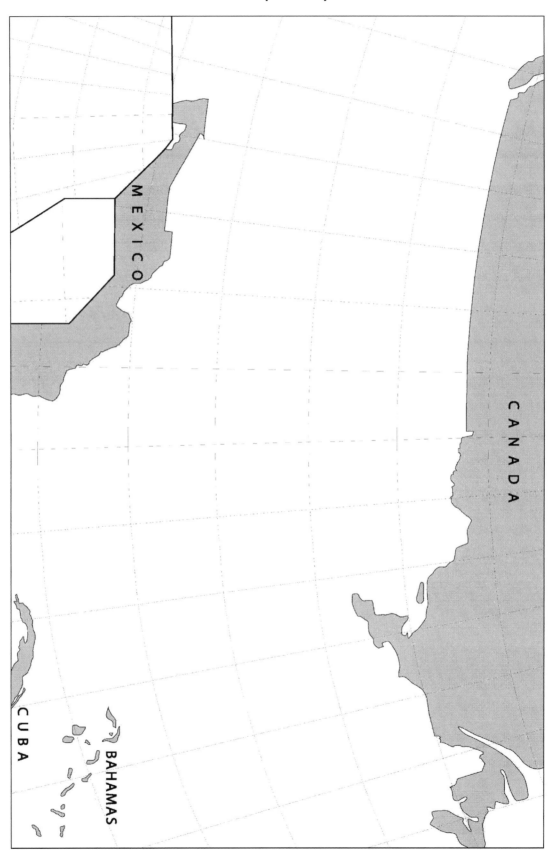

**Day 4:** On the lines below, list all of the states you have learned. On the small line, write the state abbreviation.

**Day 4:** On the map below, draw and label all of the states and capitals you have learned. Draw them without looking back.

# South Dakota

Trace the state.
Draw it in the box below.

## State Facts

| | |
|---|---|
| Capital/Abbreviation | / |
| Area/Population | / |
| Statehood | |
| Bird/Flower | / |
| Industry | |
| Interesting Fact | |

# North Dakota

Trace the state.
Draw it in the box below.

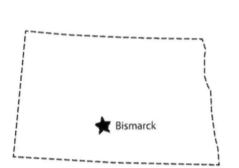

## State Facts

| | |
|---|---|
| Capital/Abbreviation | / |
| Area/Population | / |
| Statehood | |
| Bird/Flower | / |
| Industry | |
| Interesting Fact | |

**Day 1:** On the map below, trace and label
the new state and capital (or states and capitals) you have learned.

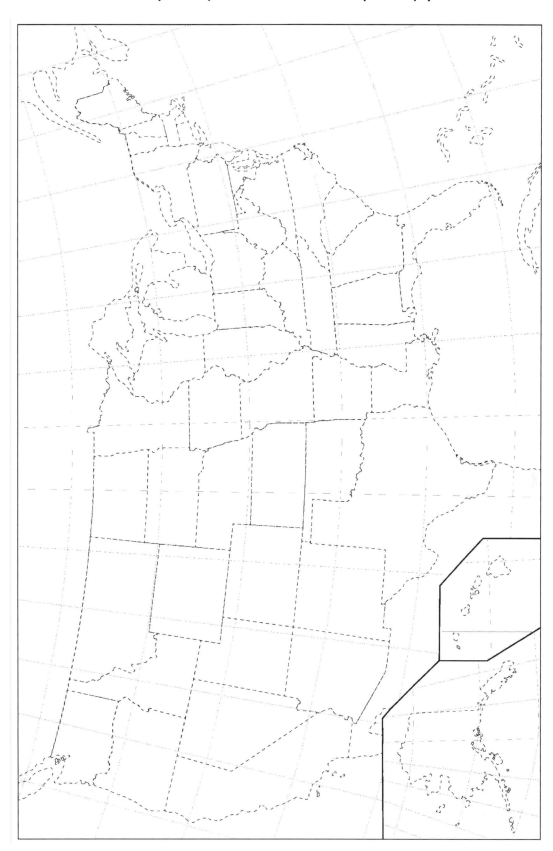

**Day 1:** On the map below, draw and label
the new state (or states) you have learned. Add the capital(s).

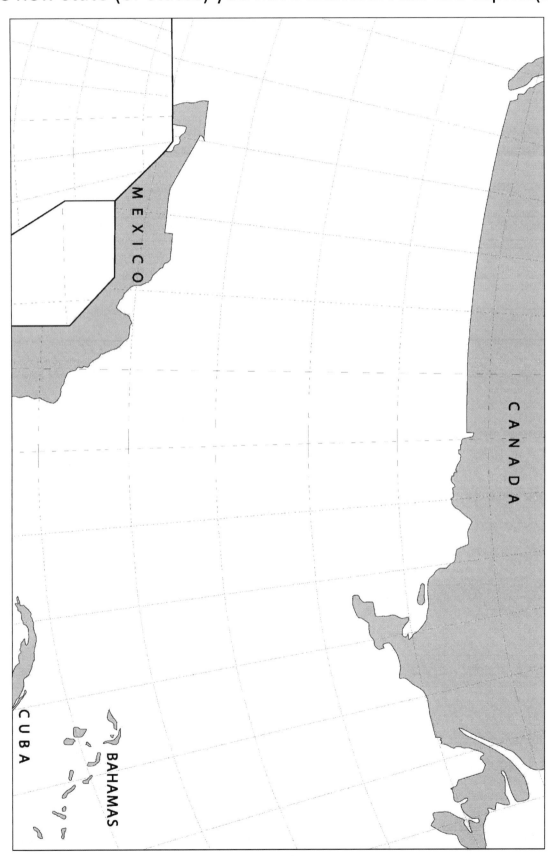

**Day 2:** On the map below, trace and label
all of the states and capitals you have learned.

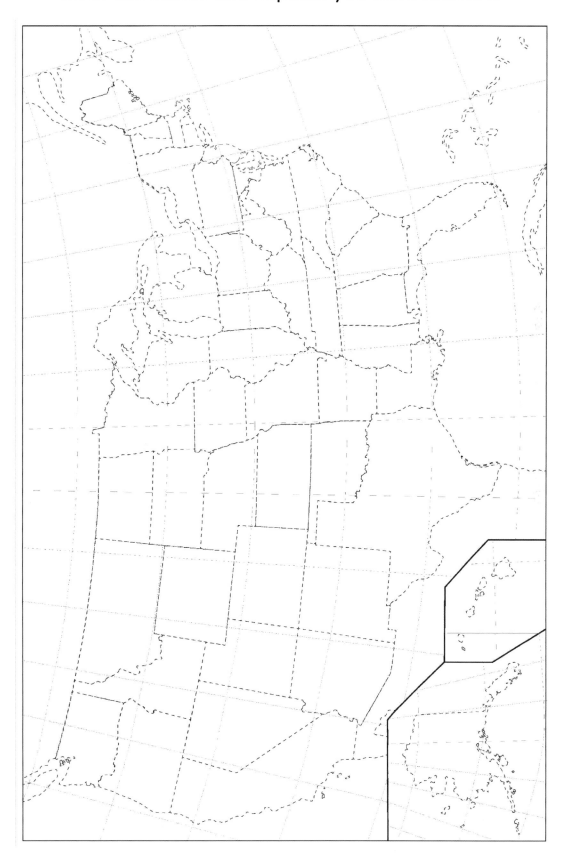

**Day 2:** On the map below, draw and label
all of the states and capitals you have learned.

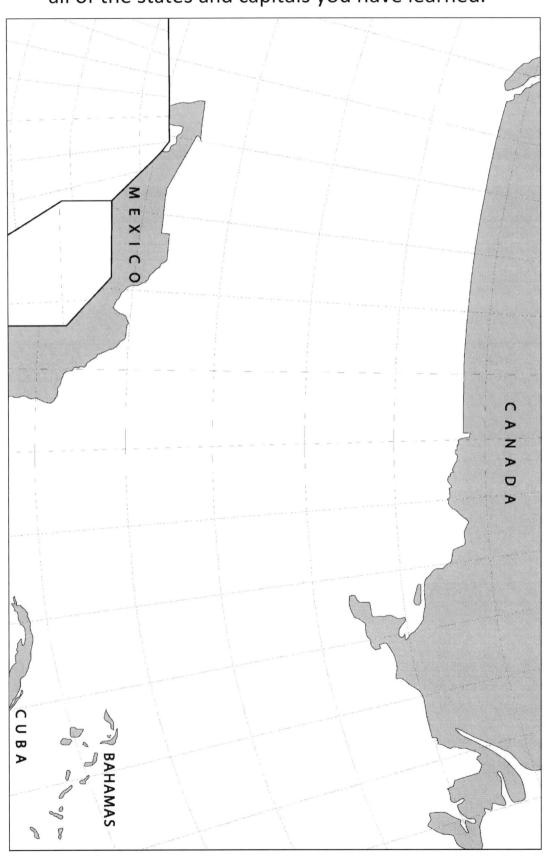

**Day 3:** On the map below, trace and label
all of the states and capitals you have learned.

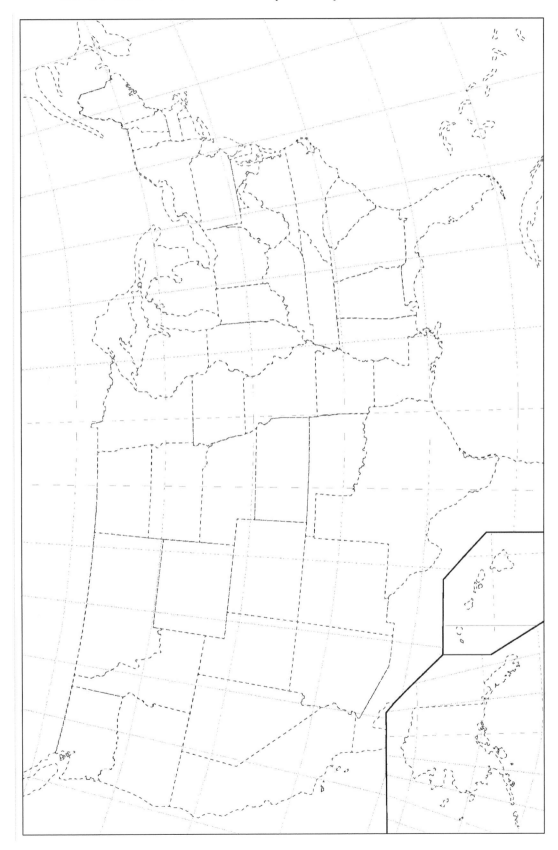

**Day 3:** On the map below, draw and label
all of the states and capitals you have learned.

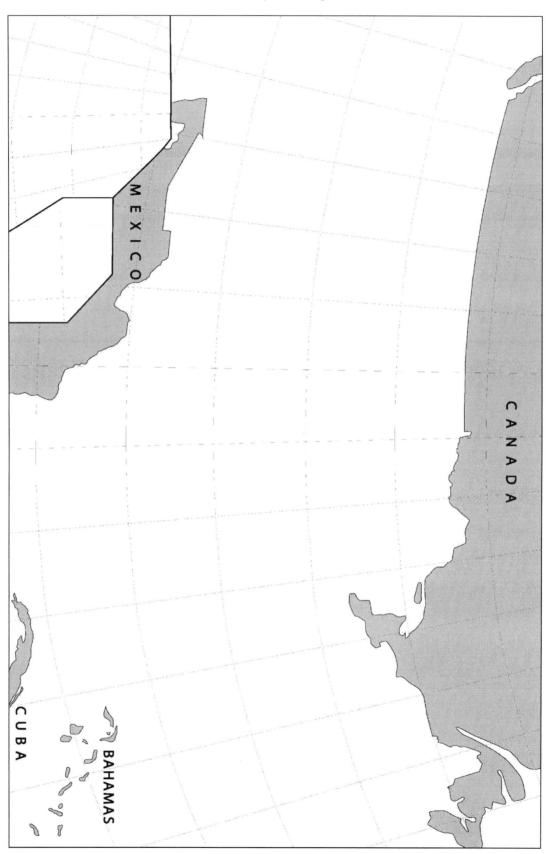

**Day 4:** On the lines below, list all of the states you have learned. On the small line, write the state abbreviation.

**Day 4:** On the map below, draw and label all of the states and capitals you have learned. Draw them without looking back.

# Montana

Trace the state.
Draw it in the box below.

## State Facts

| | |
|---|---|
| Capital/Abbreviation | / |
| Area/Population | / |
| Statehood | |
| Bird/Flower | / |
| Industry | |
| Interesting Fact | |

# Wyoming

Trace the state.
Draw it in the box below.

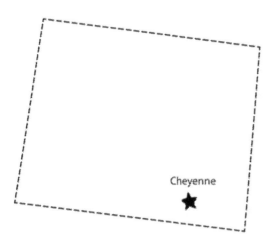

Cheyenne

## State Facts

| | |
|---|---|
| Capital/Abbreviation | / |
| Area/Population | / |
| Statehood | |
| Bird/Flower | / |
| Industry | |
| Interesting Fact | |

**Day 1:** On the map below, trace and label
the new state and capital (or states and capitals) you have learned.

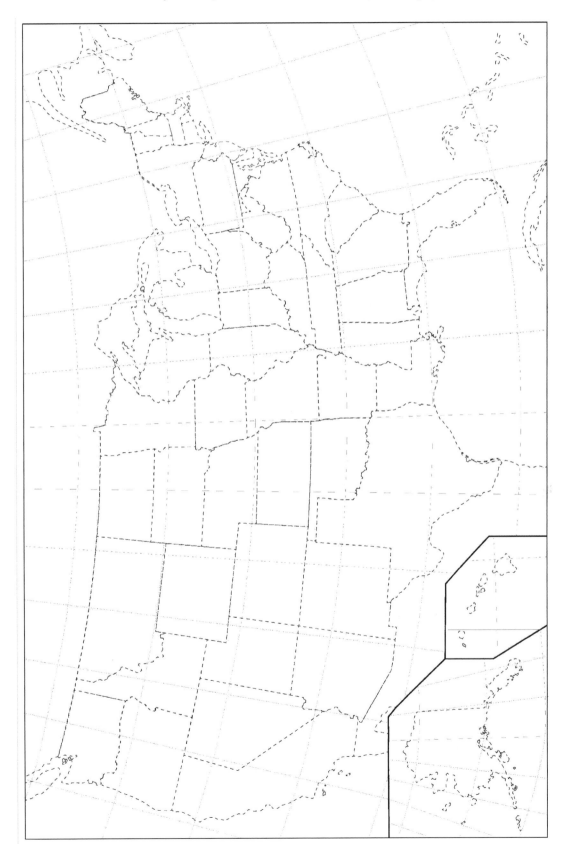

**Day 1:** On the map below, draw and label
the new state (or states) you have learned. Add the capital(s).

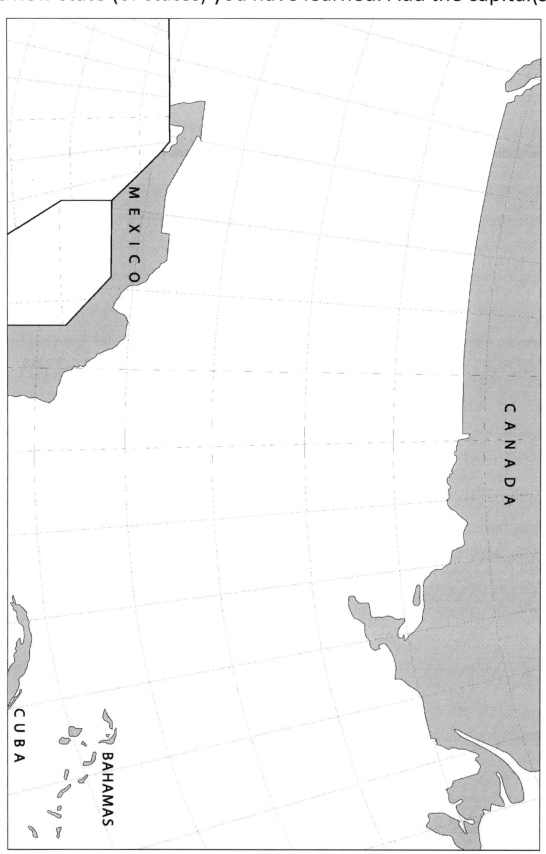

**Day 2:** On the map below, trace and label
all of the states and capitals you have learned.

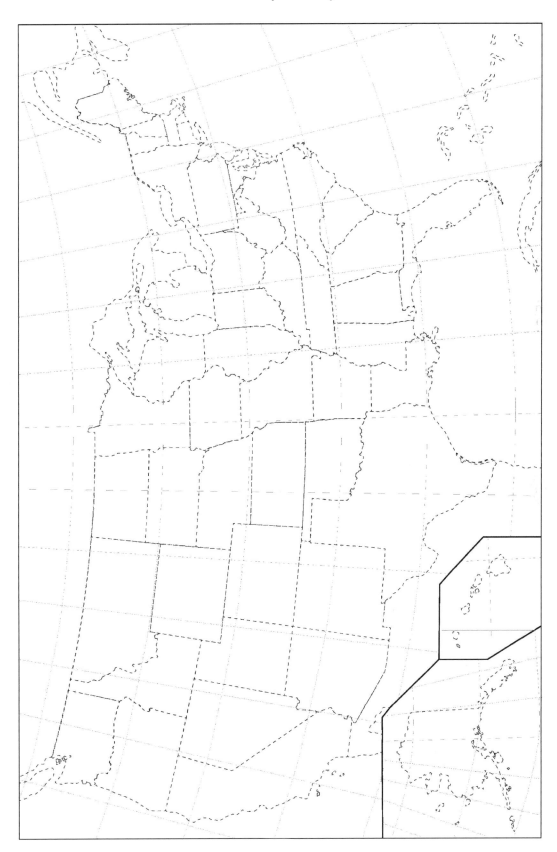

**Day 2:** On the map below, draw and label all of the states and capitals you have learned.

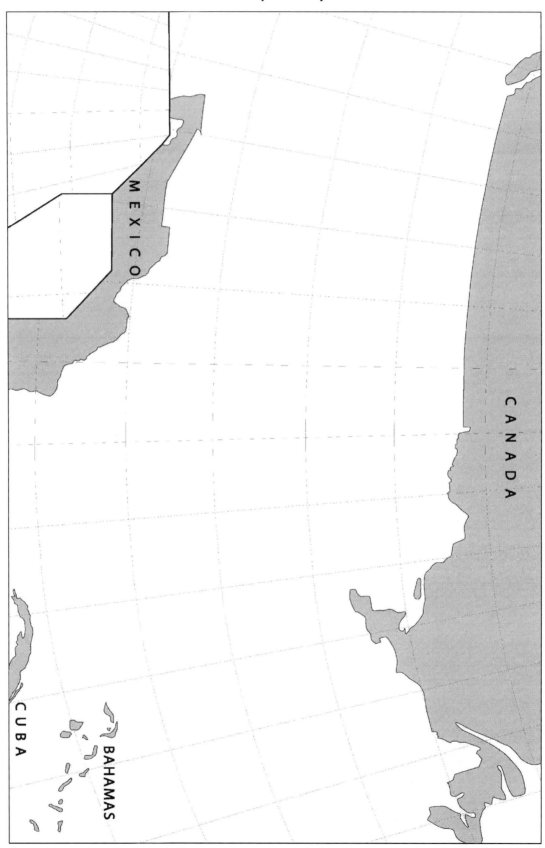

**Day 3:** On the map below, trace and label
all of the states and capitals you have learned.

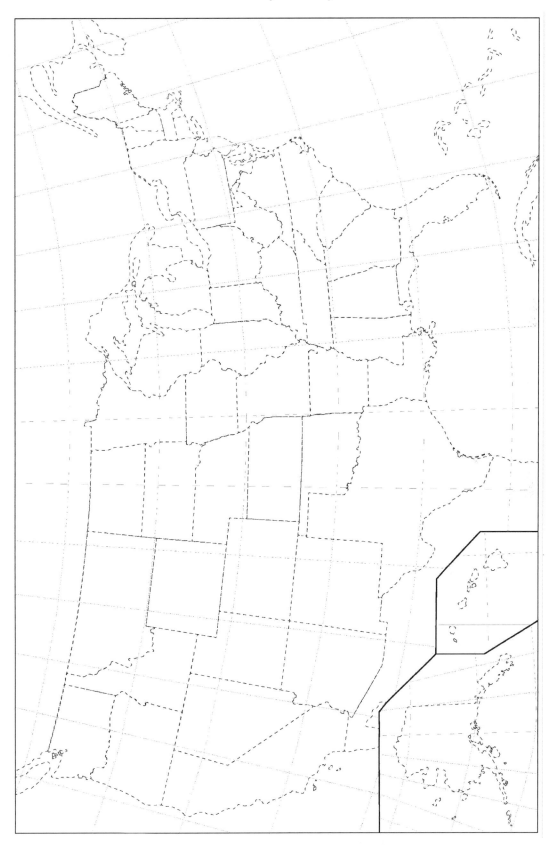

**Day 3:** On the map below, draw and label
all of the states and capitals you have learned.

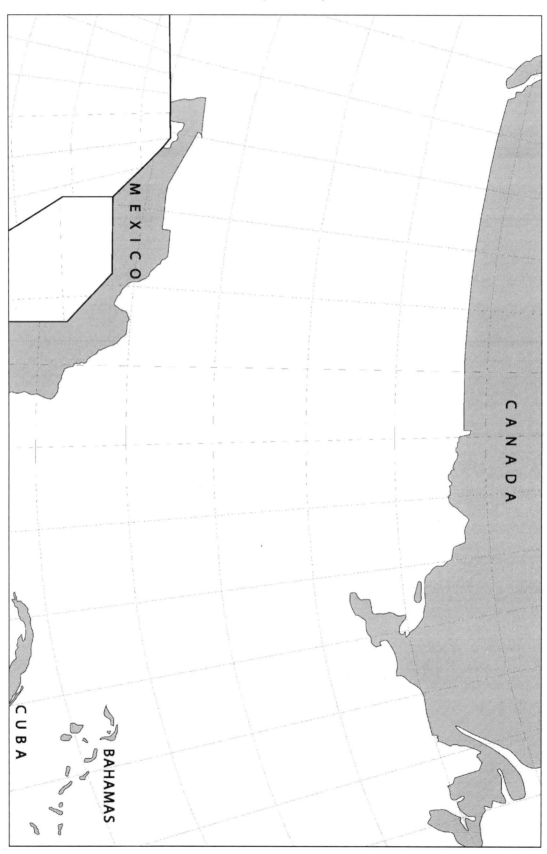

**Day 4:** On the lines below, list all of the states you have learned. On the small line, write the state abbreviation.

**Day 4:** On the map below, draw and label all of the states and capitals you have learned. Draw them without looking back.

# Colorado

Trace the state.
Draw it in the box below.

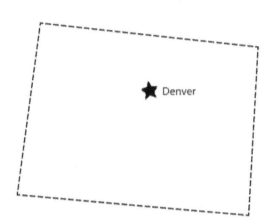

## State Facts

| | |
|---|---|
| Capital/Abbreviation | / |
| Area/Population | / |
| Statehood | |
| Bird/Flower | / |
| Industry | |
| Interesting Fact | |

# New Mexico

Trace the state.
Draw it in the box below.

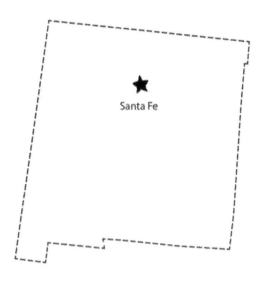

## State Facts

| | |
|---|---|
| Capital/Abbreviation | / |
| Area/Population | / |
| Statehood | |
| Bird/Flower | / |
| Industry | |
| Interesting Fact | |

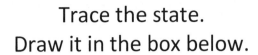

Arizona

Trace the state.
Draw it in the box below.

Phoenix

## State Facts

| | |
|---|---|
| Capital/Abbreviation | / |
| Area/Population | / |
| Statehood | |
| Bird/Flower | / |
| Industry | |
| Interesting Fact | |

## Utah

Trace the state.
Draw it in the box below.

Salt Lake City

## State Facts

| | |
|---|---|
| Capital/Abbreviation | / |
| Area/Population | / |
| Statehood | |
| Bird/Flower | / |
| Industry | |
| Interesting Fact | |

**Day 1:** On the map below, trace and label
the new state and capital (or states and capitals) you have learned.

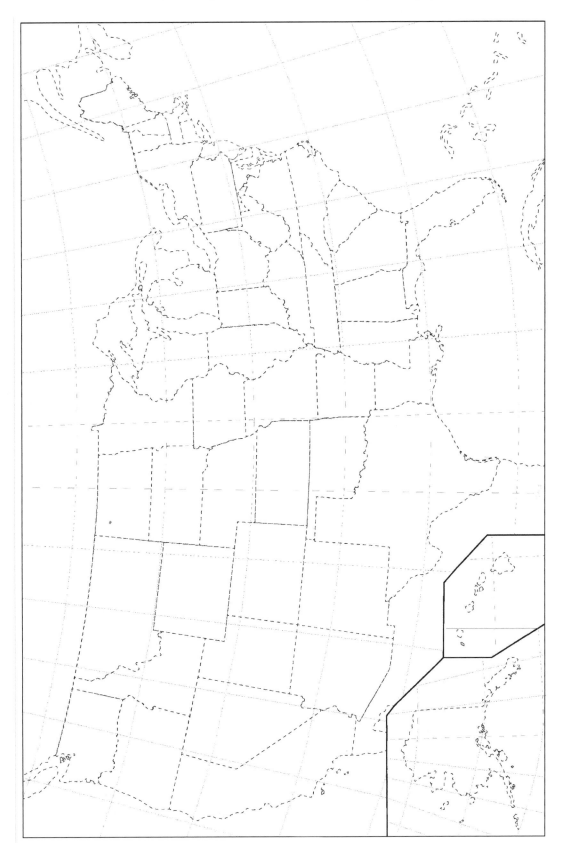

**Day 1:** On the map below, draw and label
the new state (or states) you have learned. Add the capital(s).

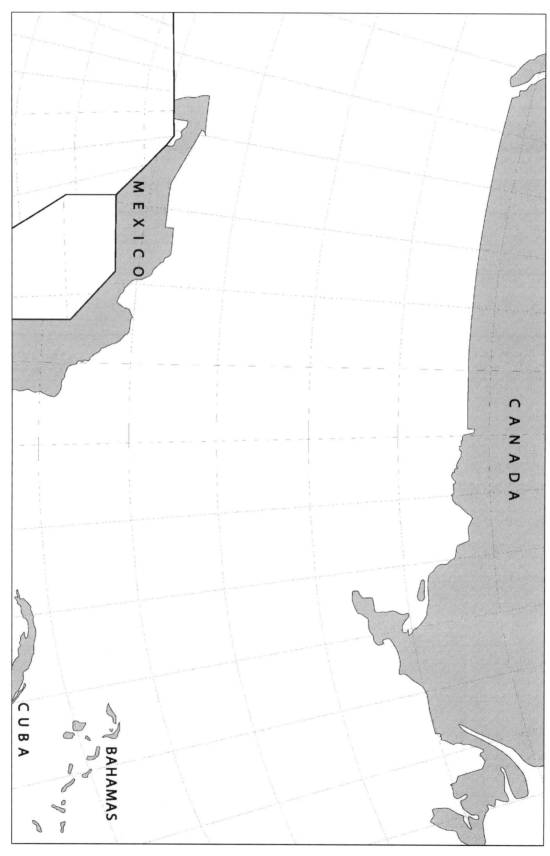

**Day 2:** On the map below, trace and label
all of the states and capitals you have learned.

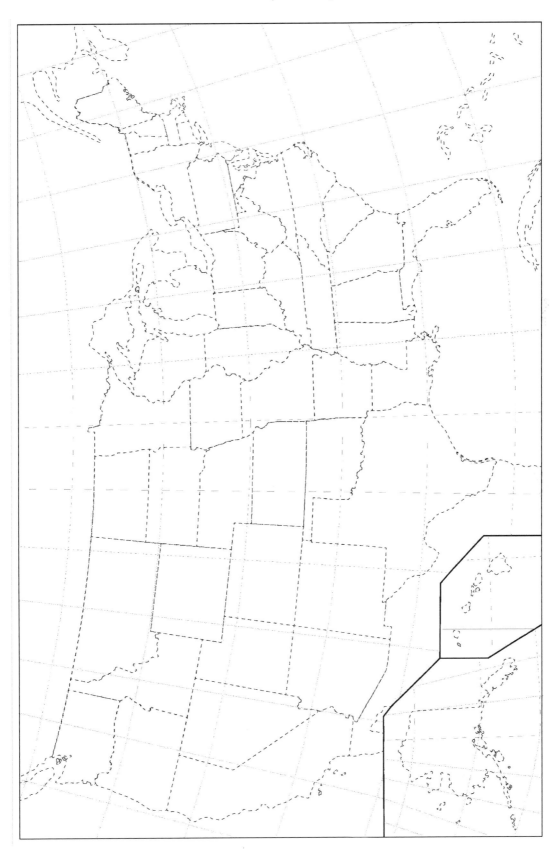

**Day 2:** On the map below, draw and label
all of the states and capitals you have learned.

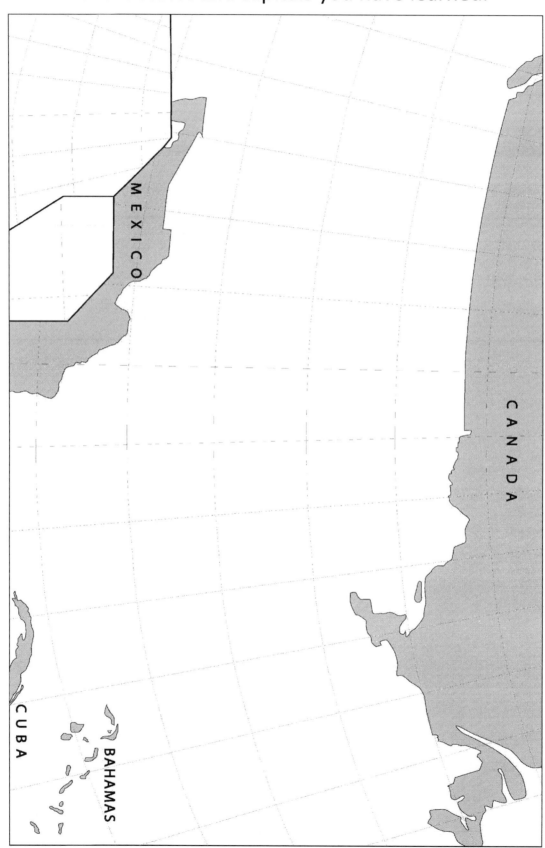

**Day 3:** On the map below, trace and label
all of the states and capitals you have learned.

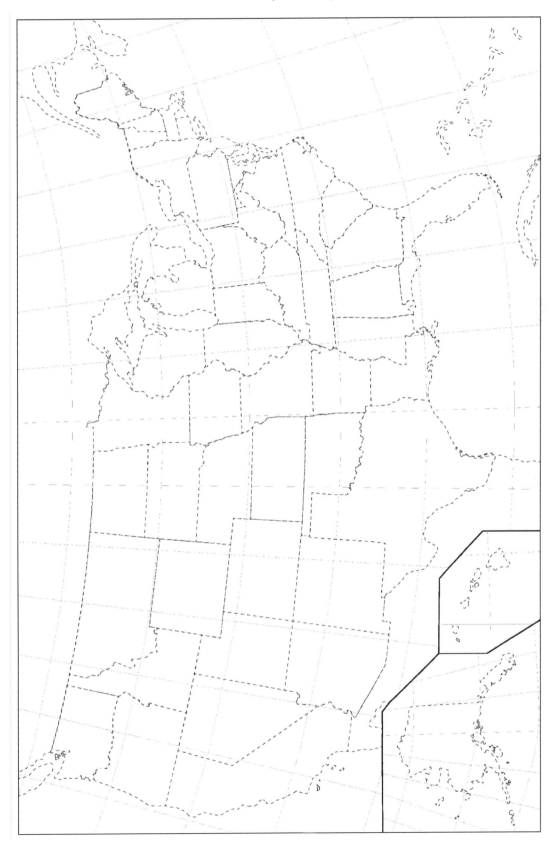

**Day 3:** On the map below, draw and label
all of the states and capitals you have learned.

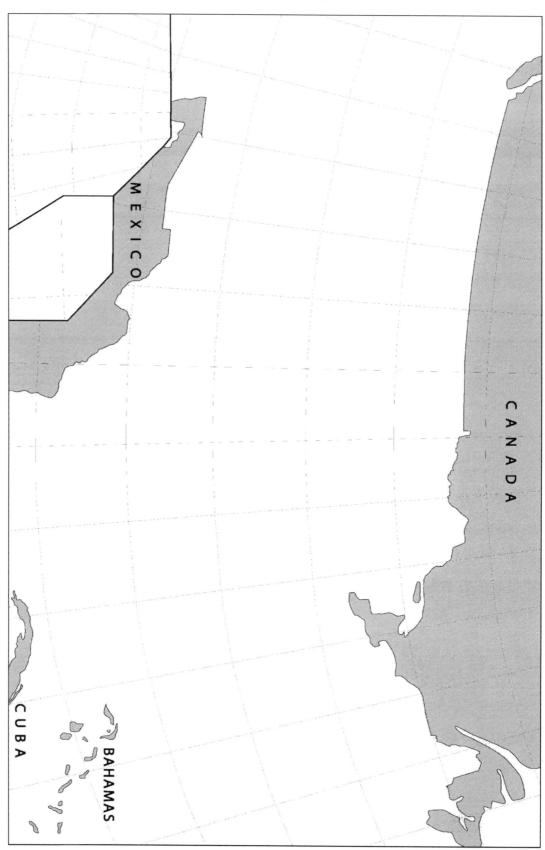

**Day 4:** On the lines below, list all of the states you have learned. On the small line, write the state abbreviation.

**Day 4:** On the map below, draw and label all of the states and capitals you have learned. Draw them without looking back.

# Idaho

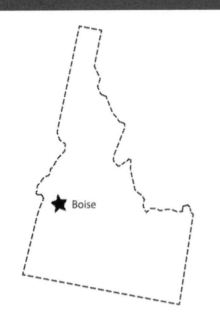

Trace the state.
Draw it in the box below.

## State Facts

| | |
|---|---|
| Capital/Abbreviation | / |
| Area/Population | / |
| Statehood | |
| Bird/Flower | / |
| Industry | |
| Interesting Fact | |

# Washington

Trace the state.
Draw it in the box below.

## State Facts

| | |
|---|---|
| Capital/Abbreviation | / |
| Area/Population | / |
| Statehood | |
| Bird/Flower | / |
| Industry | |
| Interesting Fact | |

# Oregon

Trace the state.
Draw it in the box below.

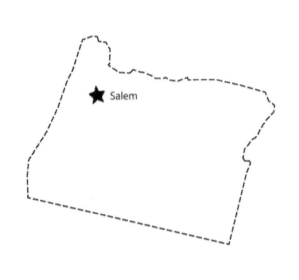

Salem

## State Facts

| Capital/Abbreviation | / |
|---|---|
| Area/Population | / |
| Statehood | |
| Bird/Flower | / |
| Industry | |
| Interesting Fact | |

**Day 1:** On the map below, trace and label
the new state and capital (or states and capitals) you have learned.

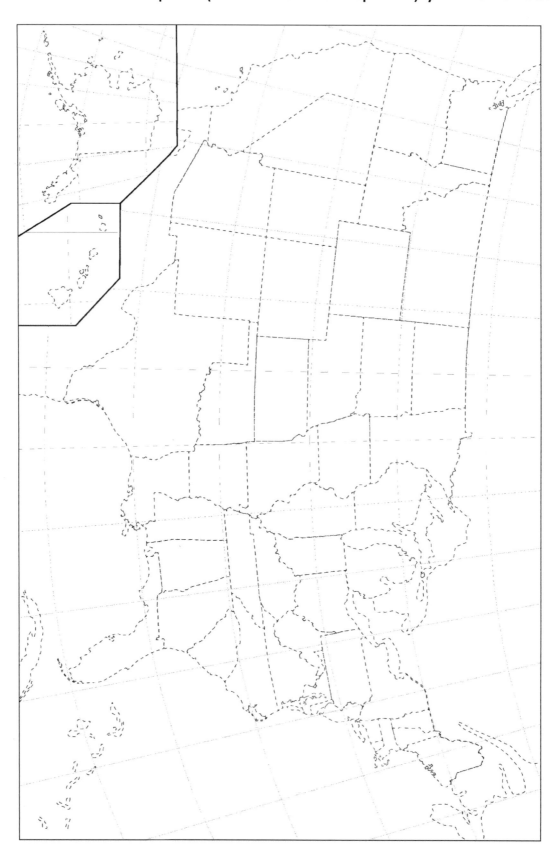

**Day 1:** On the map below, draw and label
the new state (or states) you have learned. Add the capital(s).

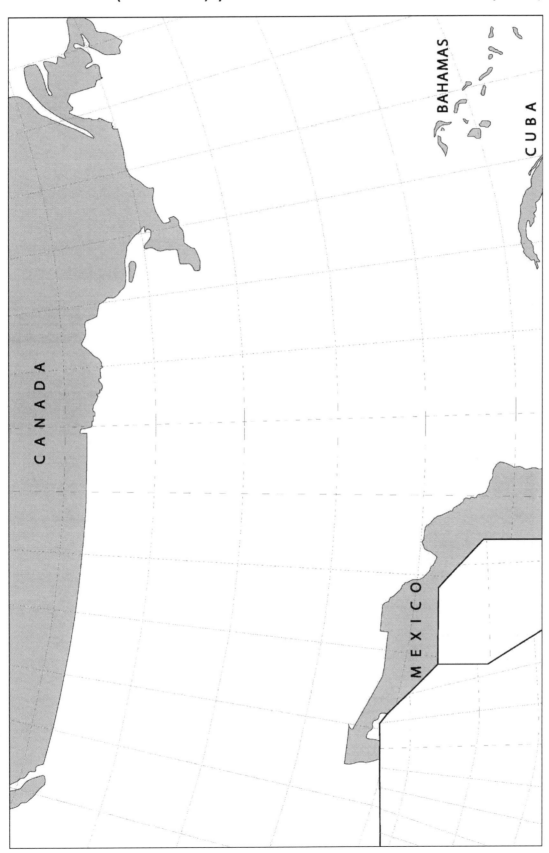

**Day 2:** On the map below, trace and label
all of the states and capitals you have learned.

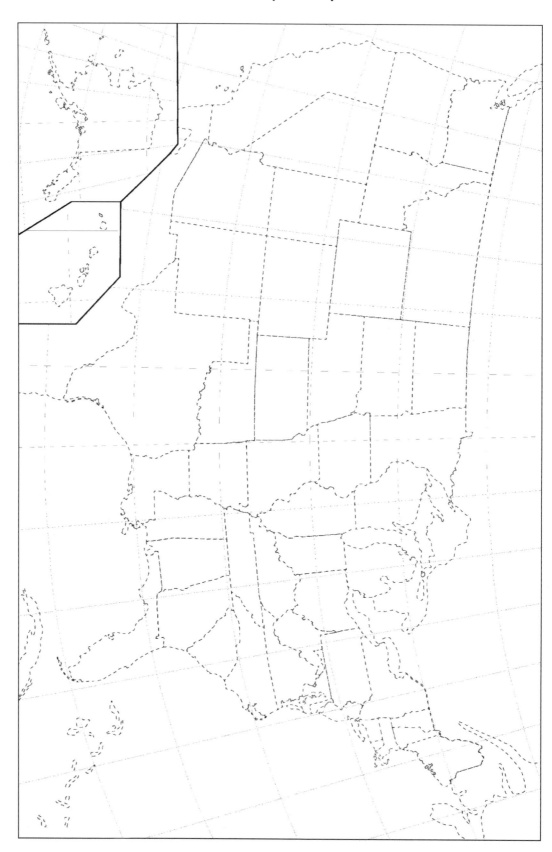

**Day 2:** On the map below, draw and label all of the states and capitals you have learned.

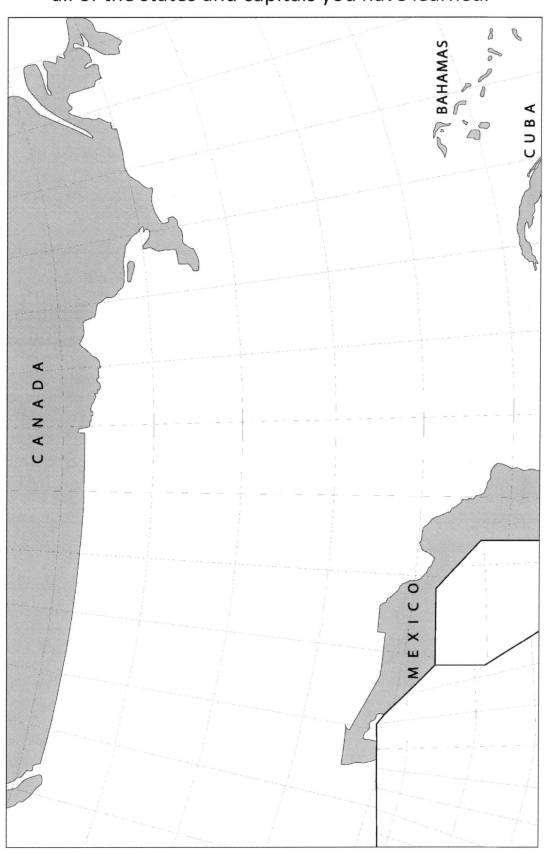

**Day 3:** On the map below, trace and label all of the states and capitals you have learned.

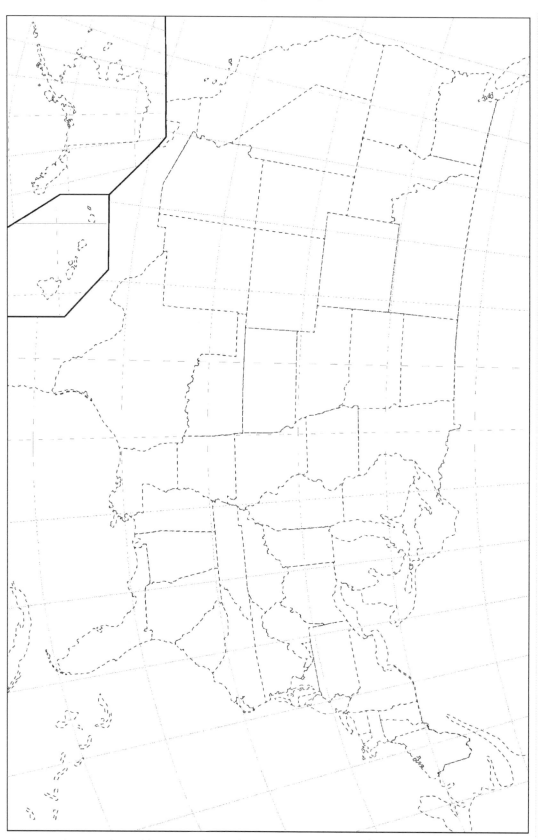

**Day 3:** On the map below, draw and label
all of the states and capitals you have learned.

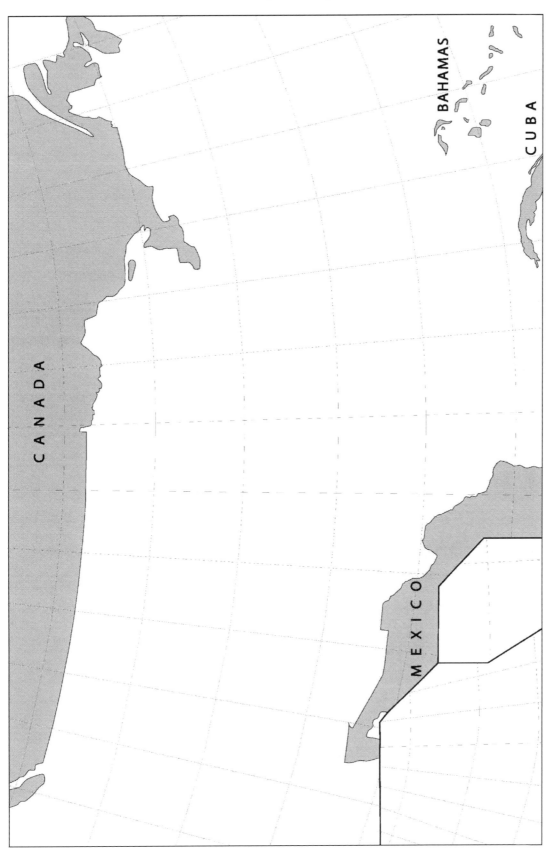

**Day 4:** On the lines below, list all of the states you have learned. On the small line, write the state abbreviation.

**Day 4:** On the map below, draw and label all of the states and capitals you have learned. Draw them without looking back.

# Nevada

Carson City

Trace the state.
Draw it in the box below.

## State Facts

| | |
|---|---|
| Capital/Abbreviation | / |
| Area/Population | / |
| Statehood | |
| Bird/Flower | / |
| Industry | |
| Interesting Fact | |

# California

Sacramento

Trace the state.
Draw it in the box below.

## State Facts

| | |
|---|---|
| Capital/Abbreviation | / |
| Area/Population | / |
| Statehood | |
| Bird/Flower | / |
| Industry | |
| Interesting Fact | |

**Day 1:** On the map below, trace and label
the new state and capital (or states and capitals) you have learned.

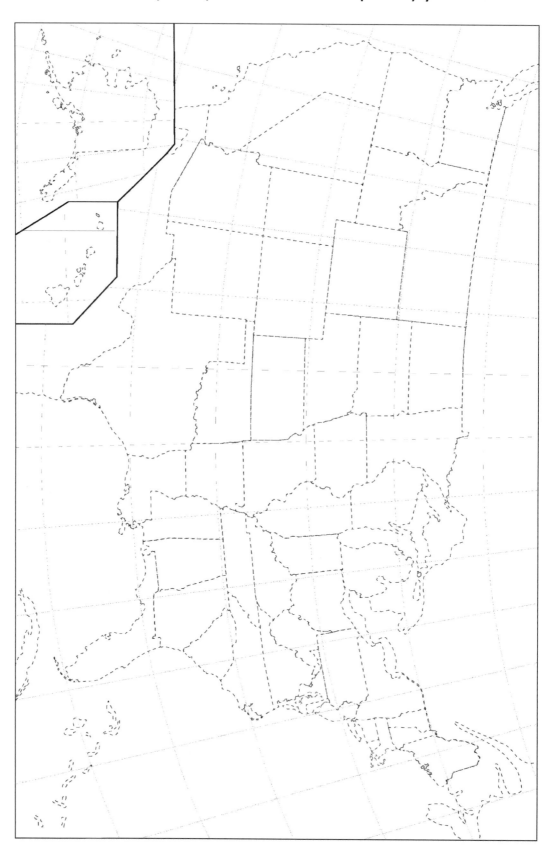

**Day 1:** On the map below, draw and label
the new state (or states) you have learned. Add the capital(s).

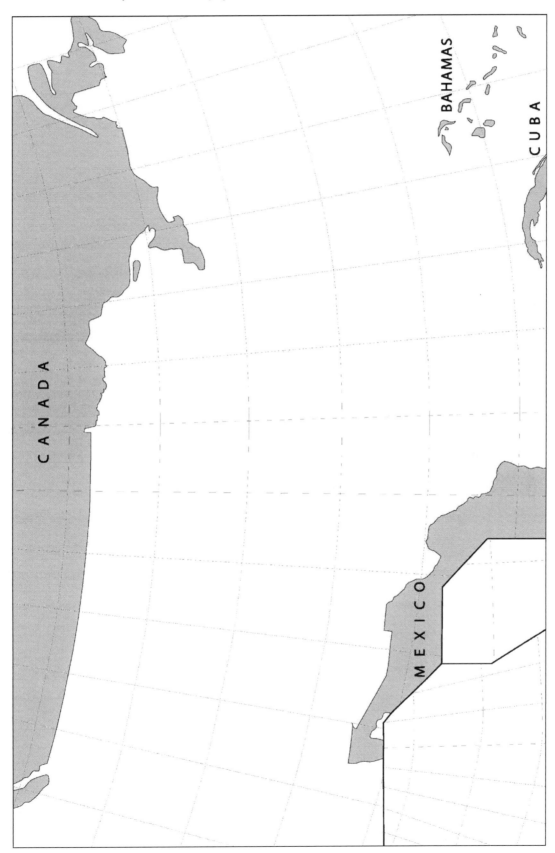

**Day 2:** On the map below, trace and label
all of the states and capitals you have learned.

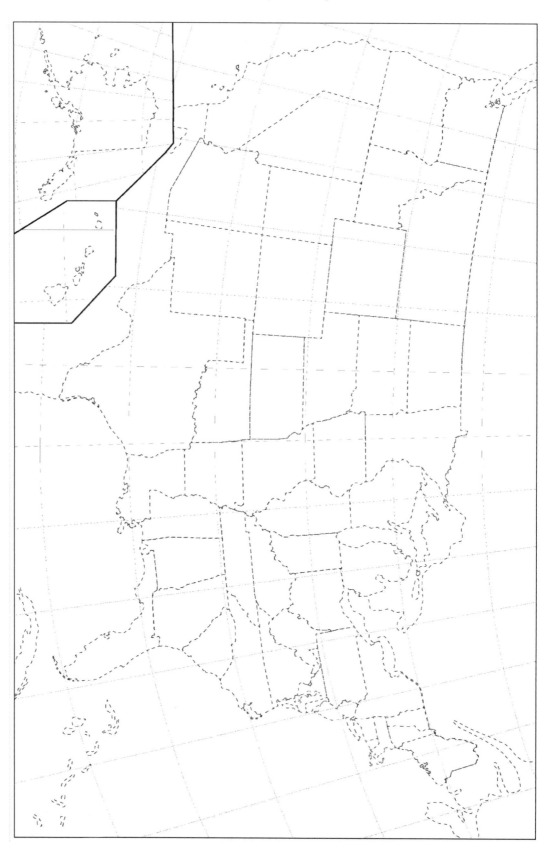

**Day 2:** On the map below, draw and label
all of the states and capitals you have learned.

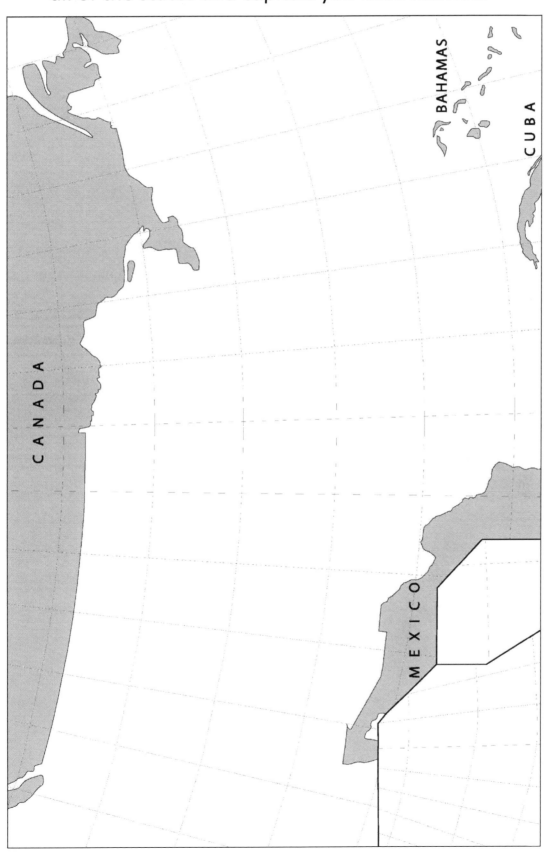

**Day 3:** On the map below, trace and label
all of the states and capitals you have learned.

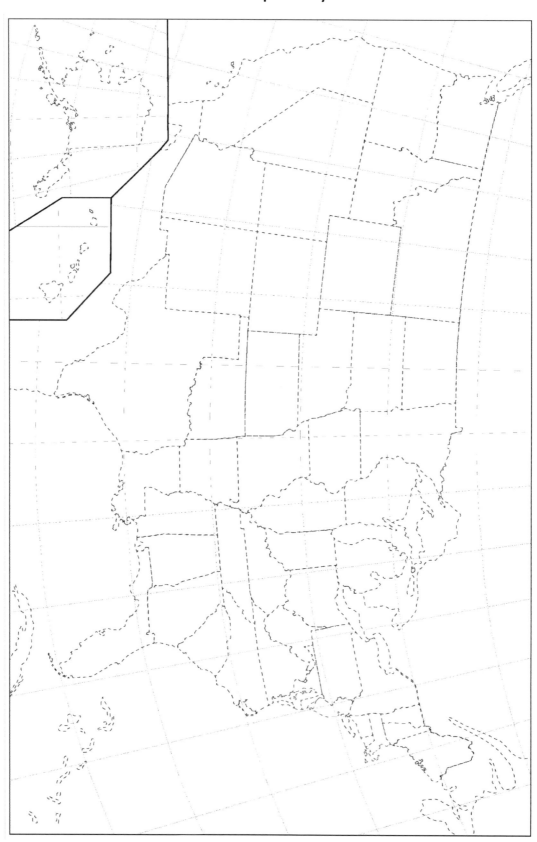

**Day 3:** On the map below, draw and label
all of the states and capitals you have learned.

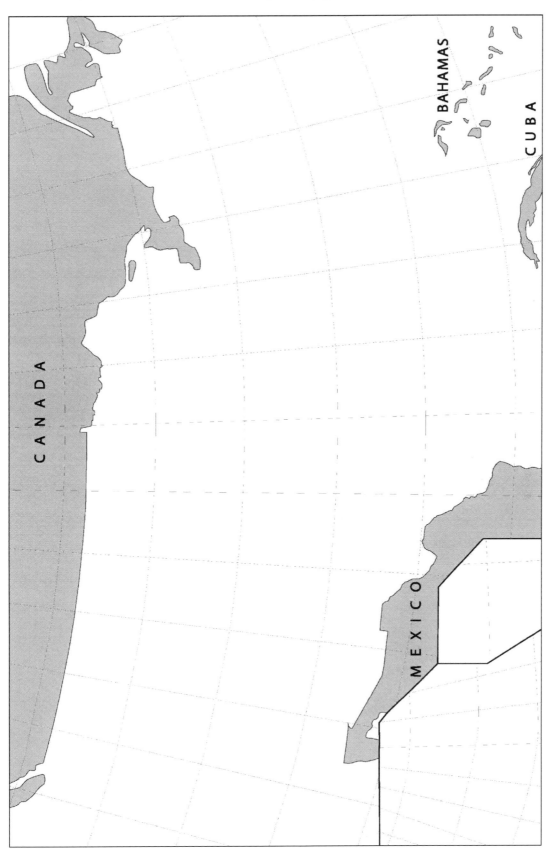

**Day 4:** On the lines below, list all of the states you have learned. On the small line, write the state abbreviation.

**Day 4:** On the map below, draw and label all of the states and capitals you have learned. Draw them without looking back.

# Alaska

Trace the state.
Draw it in the box below.

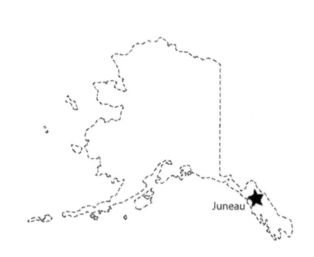

Juneau

## State Facts

| | |
|---|---|
| Capital/Abbreviation | / |
| Area/Population | / |
| Statehood | |
| Bird/Flower | / |
| Industry | |
| Interesting Fact | |

# Hawaii

Trace the state.
Draw it in the box below.

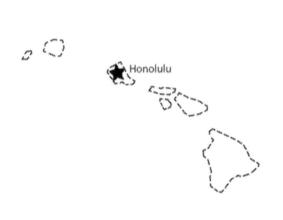

## State Facts

| | |
|---|---|
| Capital/Abbreviation | / |
| Area/Population | / |
| Statehood | |
| Bird/Flower | / |
| Industry | |
| Interesting Fact | |

# Day 1: On the map below, trace and label the new state and capital (or states and capitals) you have learned.

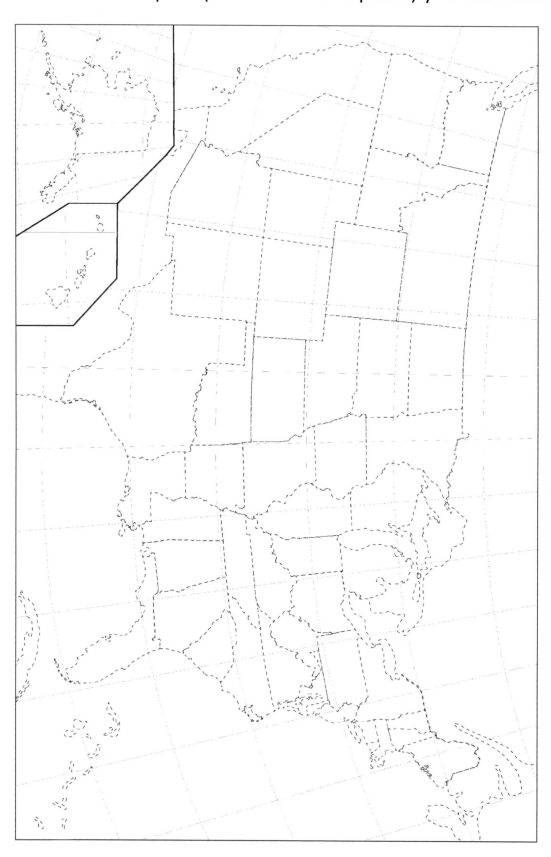

**Day 1:** On the map below, draw and label the new state (or states) you have learned. Add the capital(s).

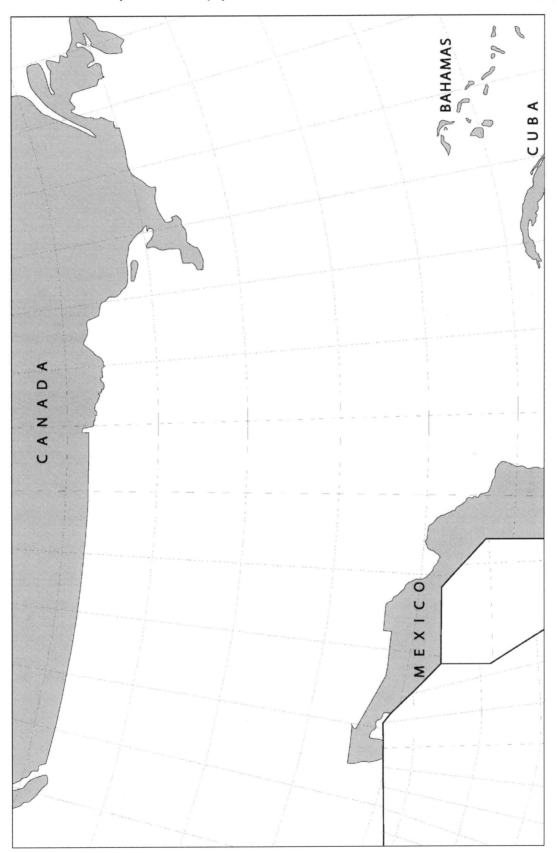

**Day 2:** On the map below, trace and label
all of the states and capitals you have learned.

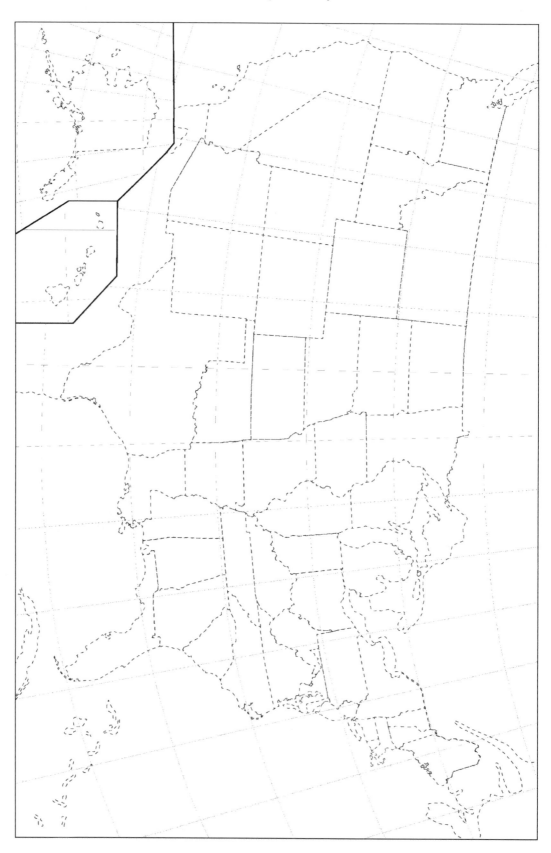

**Day 2:** On the map below, draw and label
all of the states and capitals you have learned.

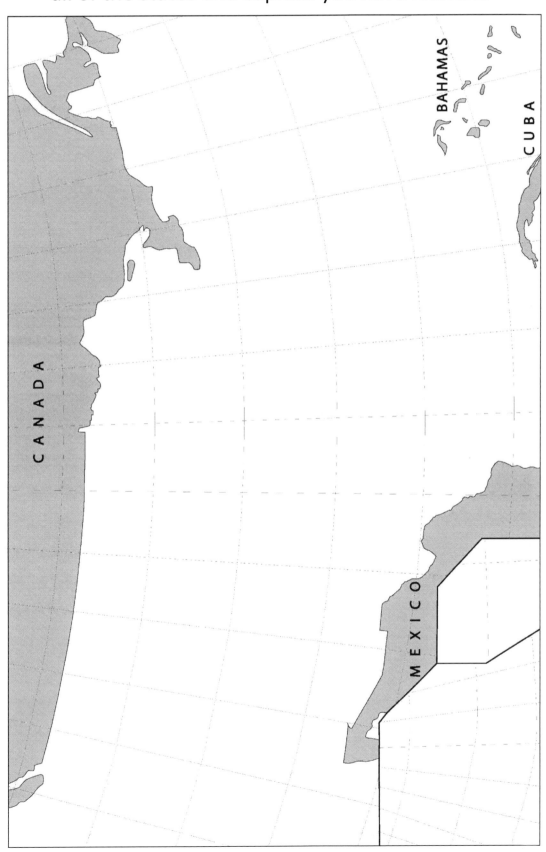

**Day 3:** On the map below, trace and label
all of the states and capitals you have learned.

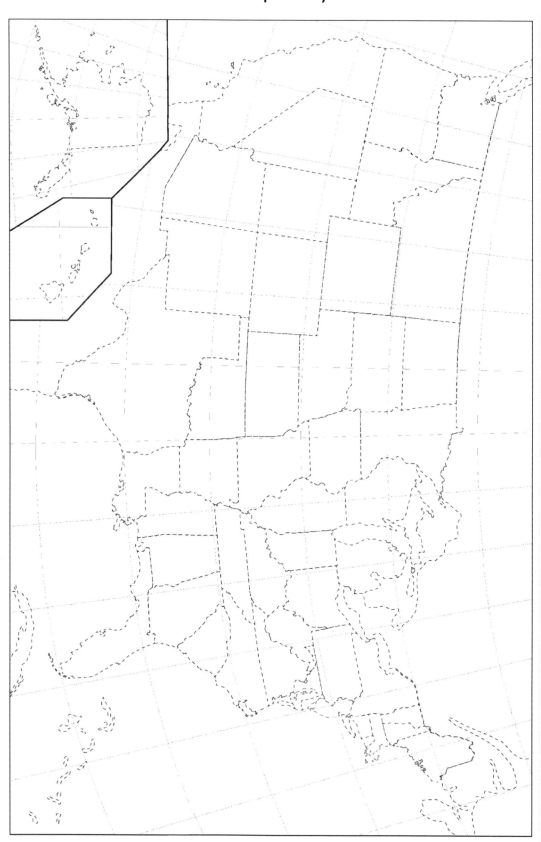

**Day 3:** On the map below, draw and label
all of the states and capitals you have learned.

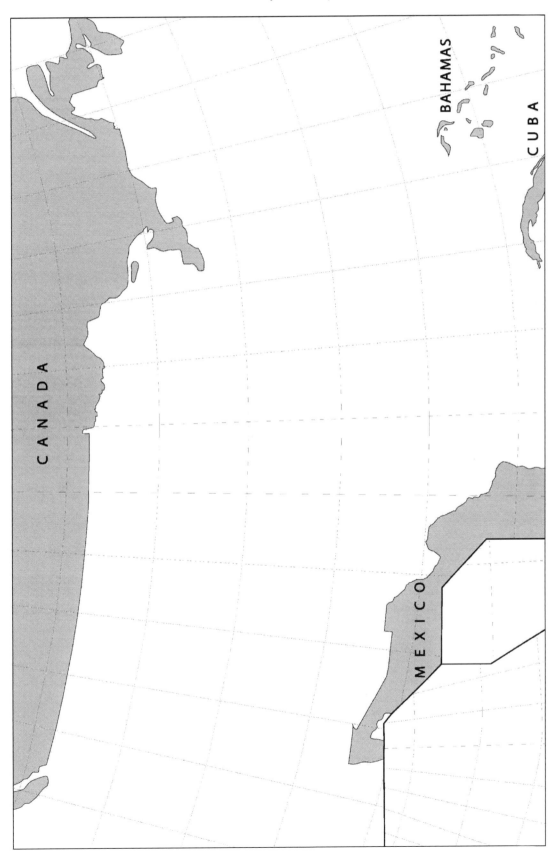

**Day 4:** On the lines below, list all of the states you have learned. On the small line, write the state abbreviation.

_____ ____    _____ ____

_____ ____    _____ ____

_____ ____    _____ ____

_____ ____    _____ ____

_____ ____    _____ ____

_____ ____    _____ ____

_____ ____    _____ ____

_____ ____    _____ ____

_____ ____    _____ ____

_____ ____    _____ ____

_____ ____    _____ ____

_____ ____    _____ ____

_____ ____    _____ ____

_____ ____    _____ ____

_____ ____    _____ ____

_____ ____    _____ ____

_____ ____    _____ ____

_____ ____    _____ ____

_____ ____    _____ ____

_____ ____    _____ ____

_____ ____    _____ ____

_____ ____    _____ ____

_____ ____    _____ ____

**Day 4:** On the map below, draw and label all of the states and capitals you have learned. Draw them without looking back.

Made in the USA
Middletown, DE
23 November 2016